V. T. Barnwell

Wreath of Gems

strictly favorite songs and tunes for the Sunday school, and for general use

in public and social worship

V. T. Barnwell

Wreath of Gems

strictly favorite songs and tunes for the Sunday school, and for general use in public and social worship

ISBN/EAN: 9783337265854

Printed in Europe, USA, Canada, Australia, Japan

Cover: Foto ©Lupo / pixelio.de

More available books at **www.hansebooks.com**

THE
WREATH OF GEMS;

OR,

STRICTLY FAVORITE SONGS AND TUNES

FOR THE

Sunday School,

AND FOR GENERAL USE IN

PUBLIC AND SOCIAL WORSHIP.

BY

V. T. BARNWELL.

NEW YORK:
Published by WM. A. POND & CO., 25 Union Square.
For sale by Booksellers generally.

ATLANTA, GEO.:
J. J. & S. P RICHARDS.

PREFACE.

THIS work has been planned and executed to meet a strong and growing demand for a music book calculated to bring the Church and the Sunday School closer together; *i. e.* make their respective exercises more homogeneous.

It is an undeniable fact that the Sunday Schools of the day are singing one class of music, while another and a very different kind is used in the Church. Now, in just so far as the Sunday School is the " Nursery of the Church," the tendency of the Sunday School singing of the present day is to draw the Church away from the use of those old, tried, and standard Songs of Zion, which, on account of their true merit, have become so eminently popular for Church purposes.

We would not advocate a too radical change in the style of Sunday School music—we would not rob the School of any life and vigor derived from cheerful music of a chaste and elevating character—we would not have the children sing exclusively dull, sluggish hymn-tunes. On the other hand, we would not have the service of the Sanctuary debased by the introduction of a class of music totally unsuited to, and beneath, its solemn dignity.

What we desire is, to have the Sunday School adopt and use many of the choice, stirring Church Tunes and Hymns. The membership of the Church should, also, constantly endeavor to learn the better class of Sunday School music practiced in the School. Then may "*All the people*," old and young, come together in the Great Congregation and sing, *with one accord*, such pieces as a refined and cultivated taste may deem peculiarly adapted to the occasion.

We have, therefore, prepared this work; giving about, or nearly, the usual number of pieces found in a Sunday School music book—endeavoring to insert *absolutely nothing not practically useful*. One half of the book (the left-hand page, throughout) has been devoted to metrical tunes, (the names of which, in each metre respectively, will be found alphabetically arranged,) and the remaining pages have been filled with sparkling Sunday School music. It is hoped that not so much as *one single piece*, in the whole book, will be found uninteresting, or otherwise impracticable.

It will be readily seen that this collection is not the work of one, two, or three minds; but that its contents have been culled from the best productions of many authors of unquestionable ability, without regard to copyright expense; most of the music herein contained is, therefore, copyright property, and the public is cautioned not to use it in other collections, without first obtaining permission from the authors, or owners of the copyrights.

The music by Dr. Lowell Mason and others has been inserted by permission of Messrs. Oliver Ditson & Co., Boston, Mass.; that by W. B. Bradbury and others, by permission of Messrs. Biglow & Main, N. Y.; that by I. B. Woodbury, by permission of Messrs. F. J. Huntington & Co., N. Y. Messrs. Wm. G. Fischer, Philadelphia; Philip Phillips, N. Y.; S. Brainard's Sons, Cleveland, Ohio; W. W. Rand, Sec. Am. T. Soc., N. Y.; Lewis T. Downs, Providence, R. I.; R. M. McIntosh, Cartersville, Ga.; and Wm. A. Pond & Co., N. Y., have also kindly permitted us to use many choice pieces of which they are the respective owners of the copyright.

That this collection of Sunday School and Church music may, in the hands of zealous Superintendents and skillful Choristers, aided by discerning Pastors, be the means of accomplishing much good, is the earnest prayer of

THE AUTHOR.

The Wreath of Gems.

1.—ANTIOCH. C. M.

DODDRIDGE.   HANDEL.

1. Joy to the world—the Lord is come! Let earth receive her King; Let ev'ry heart prepare him room, And heav'n and nature sing, And heav'n and nature sing, And heav'n, and heav'n and nature sing.

2 Joy to the earth—the Saviour reigns!
  Let men their songs employ;
While fields and floods, rocks, hill, and plains,
  Repeat the sounding joy.

3 No more let sins and sorrows grow,
  Nor thorns infest the ground;
He comes to make his blessings flow
  Far as the curse is found.

4 He rules the world with truth and grace;
  And makes the nations prove
The glories of his righteousness,
  And wonders of his love.

2.—C. M.

WATTS.

1 Now let the children of the saints
  Be dedicate to God;
Pour out Thy spirit on them, Lord,
  And wash them in Thy blood.

2 Thus to the parents and their seed,
  Shall Thy salvation come;
And numerous households meet at last,
  In one eternal home.

REJOICE! REJOICE! (Concluded.)

joice, the Prince of Peace shall reign; And Zion's children then shall sing, The deserts all are
joice, the Prince of Peace shall reign; From Zion shall the law go forth, And all shall hear from
joice, the Prince of Peace shall reign, And lambs shall with the leopard play, For naught shall harm in

blossoming: Re-joice, re-joice, the promised time is coming, Re-joice, re-joice, the
south to north: Re-joice, re-joice, the promised time is coming, Re-joice, re-joice, the
Zion's way: Re-joice, re-joice, the promised time is coming, Re-joice, re-joice, the

Prince of Peace shall reign: The gos-pel ban-ner wide unfurled, Shall wave in triumph
Prince of Peace shall reign; And truth shall sit on ev-'ry hill, And blessings flow from
Prince of Peace shall reign; The sword and spear of needless worth, Shall prune the tree and

o'er the world, And ev'ry creature, bond and free, Shall hail the glorious ju-bi-lee.
ev-'ry rill, And praise shall ev'ry heart employ, And ev'ry voice shall shout with joy.
plow the earth, And peace shall smile from shore to shore, And nations learn to war no more.

5.—AUTUMN. 8s & 7s. Double. *Spanish Tune.*

1. Hail, my ev-er-blessed Jesus! Only Thee I wish to sing; To my soul Thy name is precious, Thou my Prophet, Priest, and King; Oh, what mercy flows from heaven! Oh, what joy and happiness!

Love I much? I've much forgiven,— I'm a miracle of grace!

2. Once with Adam's race in ruin,
Unconcerned in sin I lay;
Swift destruction still pursuing,
Till my Saviour passed that way:
Witness, all ye hosts of heaven,
My Redeemer's tenderness:
Love I much? I've much forgiven,—
I'm a miracle of grace!

6.—8s & 7s Double.

1 HAIL, thou once-despised Jesus!
Hail, thou Galilean King!
Thou didst suffer to release us;
Thou didst free salvation bring.
Hail, thou agonizing Saviour,
Bearer of our sin and shame!
By Thy merits we find favor;
Life is given through Thy name.

2 Paschal Lamb, by God appointed,
All our sins on Thee were laid:
By almighty love anointed,
Thou hast full atonement made.
All Thy people are forgiven,
Through the virtue of Thy blood;
Opened is the gate of heaven;
Peace is made 'twixt man and God.

3 Jesus, hail! enthroned in glory,
There forever to abide;
All the heavenly host adore Thee,
Seated at Thy Father's side;
There for sinners Thou art pleading;
There Thou dost our place prepare:
Ever for us interceding,
Till in glory we appear.

4 Worship, honor, power, and blessing,
Thou art worthy to receive;
Loudest praises, without ceasing,
Meet it is for us to give.
Help, ye bright angelic spirits;
Bring your sweetest, noblest lays;
Help to sing our Saviour's merits;
Help to chant Immanuel's praise.

2. Possessing Christ I all possess,
Wisdom and strength and righteousness,
And holiness complete;
Bold in His name, I dare draw nigh
Before the Ruler of the sky,
And all his justice meet.

3. There is no path to heav'nly bliss,
To solid joy or lasting peace,
But Christ, th' appointed road:
Oh, may we tread the sacred way,
By faith rejoice and praise and pray,
Till we sit down with God.

9.—C. P. M.

CHAS. WESLEY.

1. O Glorious hope of perfect love!
It lifts me up to things above;
It bears on eagles' wings;
It gives my ravished soul a taste,
And makes me for some moments feast
With Jesus' priests and kings.

2. Rejoicing now in earnest hope,
I stand, and from the mountain top,
See all the land below:
Rivers of milk and honey rise,
And all the fruits of paradise
In endless plenty grow,

3. A land of corn, and wine, and oil,
Favored with God's peculiar smile,
With every blessing blessed:
There dwells the Lord our Righteousness,
And keeps His own in perfect peace,
And everlasting rest.

Cho.—I do believe, I now believe,
That Jesus died for me;
And through His blood, His precious blood,
I shall from sin be free.

2. Hark how He groans! while nature shakes,
And earth's strong pillars bend!
The temple's veil in sunder breaks,
The solid marbles rend.

3. 'Tis done! the precious ransom's paid!
"Receive my soul!" He cries:
See where He bows his sacred head!
He bows His head, and dies!

4. But soon He'll break death's envious chain,
And in full glory shine:
O Lamb of God, was ever pain,
Was ever love, like thine?

13.—HOMEWARD BOUND.

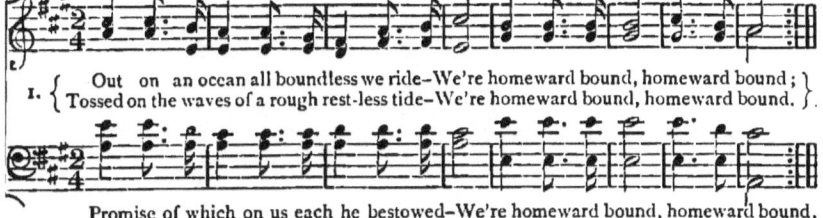

1. Out on an ocean all boundless we ride—We're homeward bound, homeward bound;
Tossed on the waves of a rough rest-less tide—We're homeward bound, homeward bound.

Promise of which on us each he bestowed—We're homeward bound, homeward bound.

Far from the safe qui-et har-bor we've rode, Seeking our Father's celes-tial a-bode,

2 Wildly the storm sweeps us on as it roars—
We're homeward bound;
Look, yonder lie the bright heavenly shores—
We're homeward bound.
Steady, O pilot, stand firm at the wheel;
Steady, we soon shall outweather the gale:
Oh how we fly 'neath the loud creaking sail—
We're homeward bound.

3 We'll tell the world as we journey along,
We're homeward bound;
Try to persuade them to enter our throng—
We're homeward bound.
Come, trembling sinner, forlorn and opprest,
Join in our number, O come and be blest;
Journey with us to the mansions of rest—
We're homeward bound.

Conclusion of words of "CONTRAST."

2 His name yields the richest perfume,
And sweeter than music his voice;
His presence disperses my gloom,
And makes all within me rejoice;
I should were he always thus nigh,
Have nothing to wish or to fear;
No mortal so happy as I,
My summers would last all the year.

3 Content with beholding his face,
My all to his pleasure resigned;
No changes of season or place,
Would make any change in my mind.

While blessed with a sense of his love,
A palace a toy would appear;
And prisons would palaces prove,
If Jesus would dwell with me there.

4 Dear Lord, if indeed I am thine,
If thou art my sun and my song,
Say why do I languish and pine?
And why are my winters so long?
O drive these dark clouds from my sky,
Thy soul-cheering presence before;
Or take me to thee up on high,
Where winter and clouds are no more.

2. Tempters assail me:
If Thou should'st fail me,
What could avail me?
Who could uphold?
But Thou hast sought me,
Found me, and bought me,
And Thou hast brought me
Unto Thy fold.—*Cho.*

3. Purest of pleasure,
Richest of treasure,
Peace without measure,
Find I in Thee.
These I inherit
By Thy good Spirit:
I have no merit;
Thou art my plea.—*Cho.*

4. Into subjection
Bring each affection,
And Thy protection
Never withhold:
Do not forsake me,
Like thyself make me;
Then, Saviour, take me
Up to Thy fold.—*Cho.*

From "Echo to H. V." By per of the Publishers.

17.—HADDAM. 6, 6, 6, 6, 8, 8.

WATTS.   DR. L. MASON.

1. The Lord Jehovah reigns, His throne is built on high; The garments he assumes Are light and majesty: His glories shine with beams so bright, No mortal eye can bear the sight.

2 The thunders of His hand
   Keep the wide world in awe:
His wrath and justice stand
   To guard His holy law;
And where His love resolves to bless,
His truth confirms and seals the grace.

3 Through all His mighty works
   Amazing wisdom shines,
Confounds the powers of hell,
   And breaks their dark designs;
Strong is His arm, and shall fulfil
His great decrees and sovereign will.

4 And will this sovereign King
   Of glory condescend?
And will He write His name
   My Father and my Friend?
I love His name, I love His word:
Join all my powers to praise the Lord.

19.—HASTINGS. 8, 6, 8, 6, 8, 8.

Rather Quick and Gliding. — HASTINGS.

1. Thou, Lord of life, whose tender care Hath led us on till now, Here, lowly, at the hour of prayer, Before Thy throne we bow: We bless Thy gracious hand, and pray Forgiveness for another day.

2. With prayer, our humble praise we bring,
For mercies day by day:
Lord, teach our hearts Thy love to sing;
Lord, teach us how to pray;
All that we have we owe to Thee,—
Thy debtors through eternity.

3. Thou, blessed God, hast been our guide,
Through life our guard and friend;
Yet still, throughout life's weary tide,

Preserve us to the end:
And when this life's sad journey's past,
Receive us to Thyself at last.

4. In our Redeemer's name, for all
These blessings we implore;
Prostrate, O Lord, before thee fall,
And gratefully adore:
Bend from Thy throne of earth and skies,
And bless our evening sacrifice.

20.—8, 6, 8, 6, 8, 8. DR. T. HASTINGS.

1. How calm and beautiful the morn
That gilds the sacred tomb,
Where once the Crucified was borne
And veiled in midnight gloom;
O! weep no more the Saviour slain,
The Lord is risen—He lives again.

2. How tranquil now the rising day—
'Tis Jesus still appears
A risen Lord, to chase away

Your unbelieving fears;
O! weep no more your comforts slain,
The Lord is risen—He lives again.

3. And when the shades of evening fall,
When life's last hour draws nigh,
If Jesus shines upon the soul,
How blissful then to die;
Since He has risen who once was slain,
Ye die in Christ to live again.

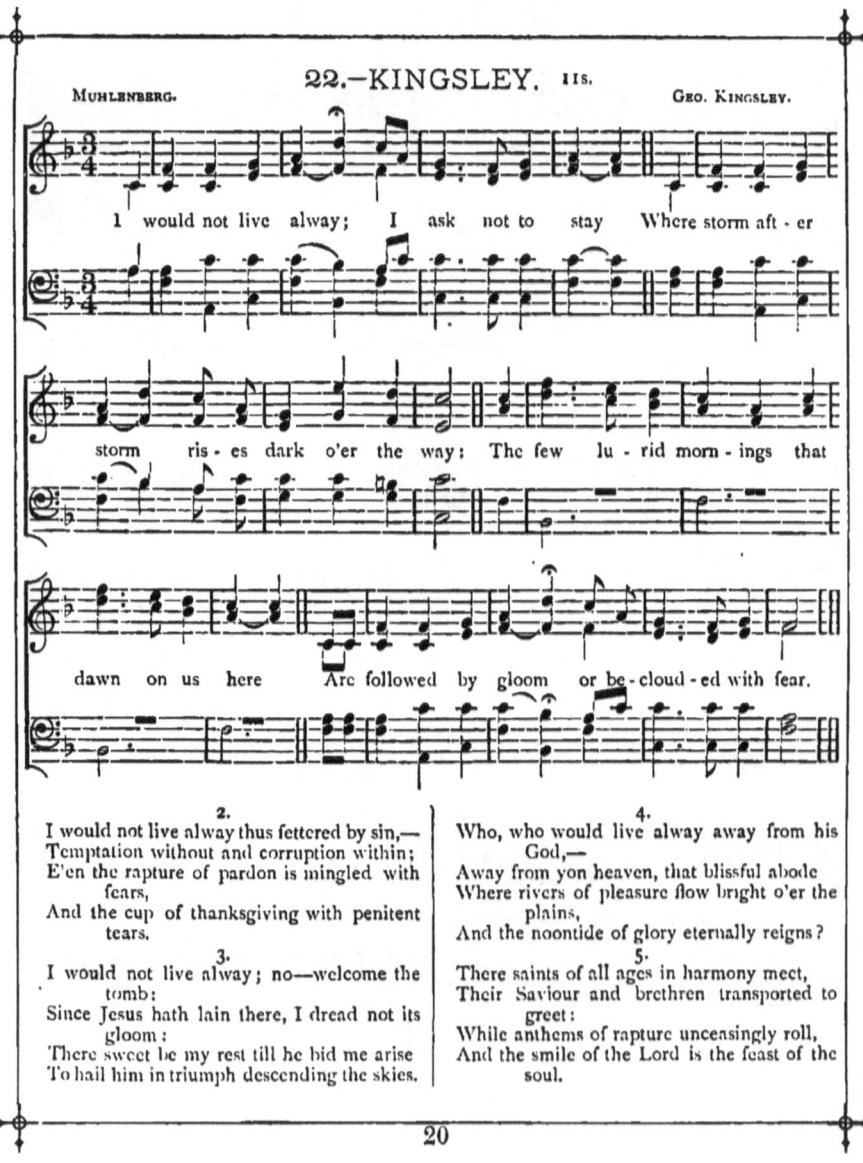

2.
I would not live alway thus fettered by sin,—
Temptation without and corruption within;
E'en the rapture of pardon is mingled with fears,
And the cup of thanksgiving with penitent tears.

3.
I would not live alway; no—welcome the tomb:
Since Jesus hath lain there, I dread not its gloom:
There sweet be my rest till he bid me arise
To hail him in triumph descending the skies.

4.
Who, who would live alway away from his God,—
Away from yon heaven, that blissful abode
Where rivers of pleasure flow bright o'er the plains,
And the noontide of glory eternally reigns?

5.
There saints of all ages in harmony meet,
Their Saviour and brethren transported to greet:
While anthems of rapture unceasingly roll,
And the smile of the Lord is the feast of the soul.

23.—HOSANNA.

1. Ho-san-na to the Son of Da-vid! The chil-dren sung of old; And thro' the ho-ly tem-ple The joy-ous anthem rolled. Ho-san-na! ho-san-na! ho-san-na in the high-est to David's roy-al Son. Ho-san-na! ho-san-na! Bless-ed is He that com-eth in the name of the Lord!

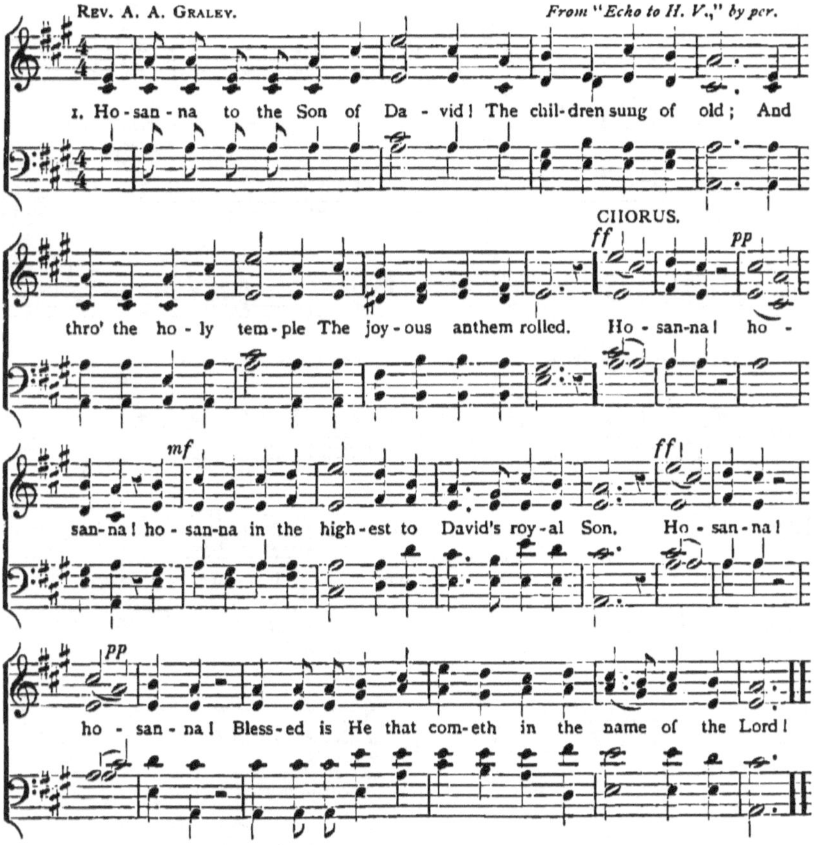

2 Hosanna to the Son of David!
   The palm of victory wave;
   Hosanna in the highest!
   He comes to bless and save!—Cho.

3 Hosanna to the Son of David!
   They sang 'mid frowns and foes;
   And louder yet, and louder,
   Their song triumphant rose.—Cho.

4 Hosanna to the Son of David!
   Our youthful lips reply;
   For us He left His glory,
   For us He came to die.—Cho.

5 Hosanna to the Son of David!
   Let every creature sing,
   And every heart enthrone Him
   As Prophet, Priest, and King.—Cho.

2 Now may the King descend,
  And fill His throne of grace;
  Thy sceptre, Lord, extend,
  While saints address Thy face:
  Let sinners feel Thy quick'ning word,
  And learn to know and fear the Lord.

3 Descend, celestial Dove,
  With all Thy quick'ning powers;
  Disclose a Saviour's love,
  And bless the sacred hours.
  Then shall my soul new life obtain,
  Nor Sabbaths be indulged in vain.

25.—SAVE, LORD, OR WE PERISH.

HEBER. V. T. BARNWELL.

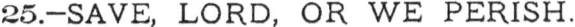

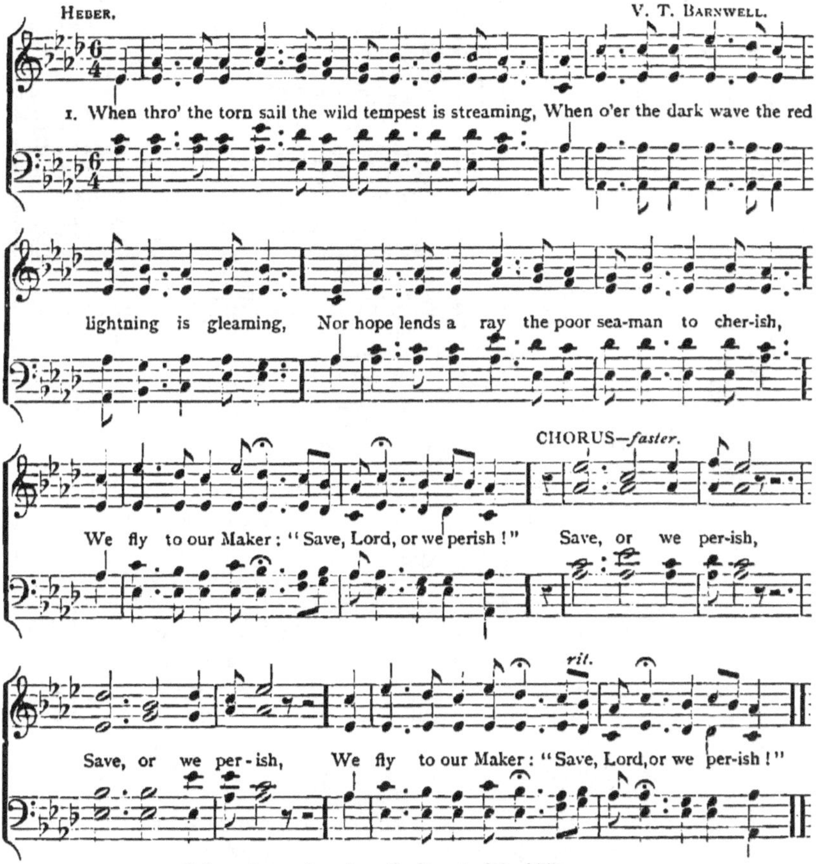
1. When thro' the torn sail the wild tempest is streaming, When o'er the dark wave the red
lightning is gleaming, Nor hope lends a ray the poor sea-man to cher-ish,
We fly to our Maker: "Save, Lord, or we perish!"
CHORUS—*faster.*
Save, or we per-ish,
Save, or we per-ish,
We fly to our Maker: "Save, Lord, or we per-ish!"
rit.

2 O Jesus! once tossed on the breast of the billow,
Aroused by the shriek of despair from Thy pillow,
Now, seated in glory, the mariner cherish,
Who cries in his danger—"Save, Lord, or we perish!"

3 And O! when the whirlwind of passion is raging,
When hell in our heart his wild warfare is waging,
Arise in Thy strength, thy redeemed to cherish,
Rebuke the destroyer—"Save, Lord, or we perish!"

CHAS. WESLEY. EDSON.

1. Blow ye the trumpet, blow, The glad-ly sol-emn sound! Let all the na-tions know, To earth's re-mot-est bound, The year of ju-bi-lee is come! Re-turn, ye ran-somed sin-ners, home; Re-turn, ye ran-somed sin-ners, home.

2 Jesus, our great High Priest,
 Hath full atonement made :
 Ye weary spirits, rest :
 Ye mournful souls, be glad :
 The year of jubilee is come !
 Return, ye ransomed sinners, home.

3 Extol the Lamb of God,
 The all-atoning Lamb ;
 Redemption in His blood
 Throughout the world proclaim :
 The year of jubilee is come !
 Return, ye ransomed sinners, home.

27.—LYONS. 10S & 11S.

FRANCIS JOSEPH HAYDN.

1. Tho' troubles as-sail, and dangers affright, Tho' friends should all fail, and foes all unite, Yet one thing secures us, whatever be-tide, The promise assures us, "The Lord will provide."

2 The birds, without barn or store-house, are fed ;
 From them let us learn to trust for our bread :
 His saints what is fitting shall ne'er be denied,
 So long as 'tis written, "The Lord will pro-
   vide."

3 When Satan appears to stop up our path,
 And fills us with fears, we triumph by faith ;
 He cannot take from us, tho' oft he has tried,
 The heart-cheering promise, "The Lord will
   provide."

28.—CHRISTMAS MORN.

Written for this work, by C. F. BARNWELL.

1. Hark! the heavenly mu-sic—An-gel voi-ces sing; And they tell to earth Immanuel's fame;
2. Peace to earth they her-ald, Christ the Lord is born, Heav'n and earth unite his praise to sing;
3. O ye mortals, serve Him, hon-or and a-dore, Chant the wondrous sto-ry of His love;

Hear the wondrous sto-ry—hear their voices ring, Shouting hal-le-lu-jahs to His name.
O, receive the message they to earth have borne, Hail your Prophet! hail your Priest and King!
Spread the joy-ful tidings, till for-ev-er more Ye shall join the an-gel hosts a-bove.

CHORUS.

Glo-ry, glo-ry, glo-ry be to God! With sweet an-gels shout in tones of joy:

rit.

Glo-ry be to Je-sus, glo-ry be to God, Glo-ry be to God—to God most high.

29.—MISSIONARY HYMN. 7s & 6s.

HEBER.   DR. L. MASON.

1. From Greenland's i-cy mountains, From In-dia's co-ral strand; Where Afric's sun-ny fount-ains Roll down their gold-en sand; From many an an-cient riv-er, From many a palm-y plain, They call us to de-liv-er Their land from error's chain.

2 What though the spicy breezes
    Blow soft o'er Ceylon's isle,
Though every prospect pleases,
    And only man is vile:
In vain with lavish kindness
    The gifts of God are strown;
The heathen in his blindness
    Bows down to wood and stone.

3 Shall we whose souls are lighted
    With wisdom from on high,
Shall we to men benighted
    The lamp of life deny?

Salvation! O, Salvation!
    The joyful sound proclaim,
Till earth's remotest nation
    Has learned Messiah's name.

4 Waft, waft, ye winds, his story,
    And you, ye waters, roll,
Till, like a sea of glory,
    It spreads from pole to pole;
Till o'er our ransomed nature
    The Lamb for sinners slain,
Redeemer, King, Creator,
    In bliss returns to reign.

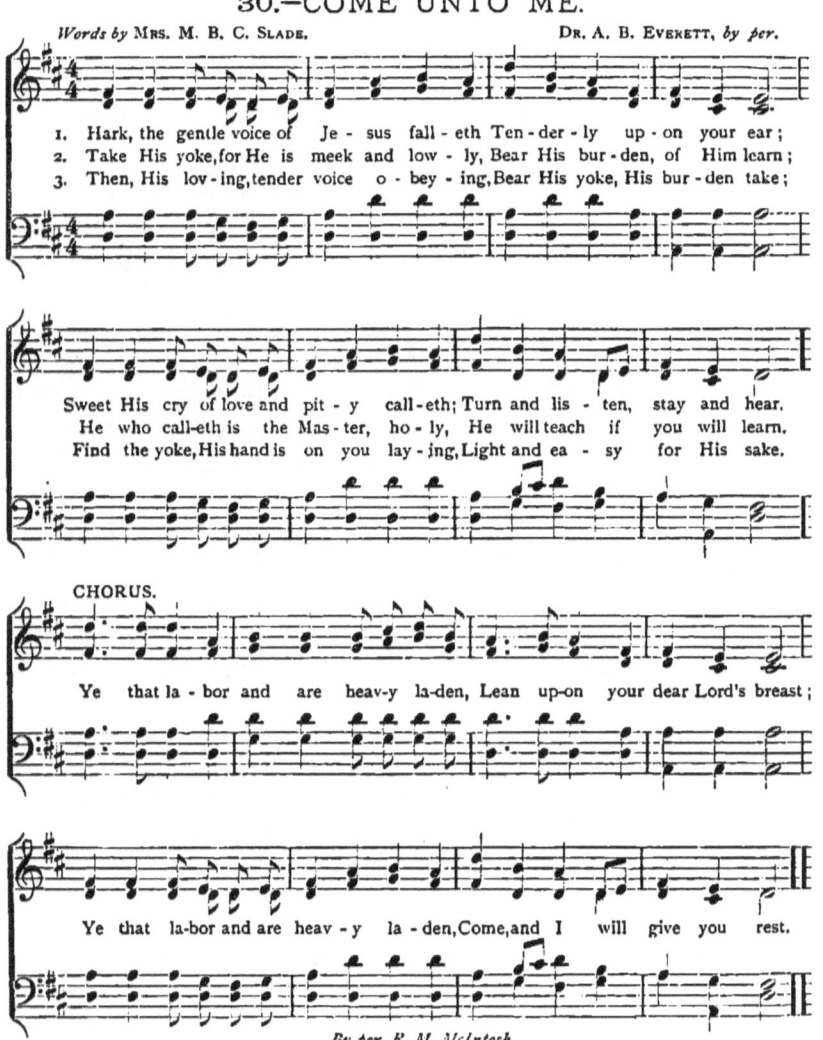

31.—NETTLETON. 8s & 7s.

H. F. Lyte.

1. Jesus, I my cross have taken, All to leave and follow Thee;
Naked, poor, despised, forsaken, Thou, from hence, my all shalt be.
Perish ev'ry fond ambition, All I've sought, or hoped, or known;
Yet how rich is my condition! God and heav'n are still my own!

*CHORUS.
I love Jesus, Hallelujah! I love Jesus, yes, I do;
I do love Jesus, He's my Saviour; And I know He loves me too.

2 Let the world despise and leave me,
They have left my Saviour, too;
Human hearts and looks deceive me—
Thou art not, like them, untrue:
And while Thou shalt smile upon me.
God of wisdom, love and might,
Foes may hate and friends disown me;
Show Thy face and all is bright.—Cho.

2 Go, then, earthly fame and treasure;
Come, disaster, scorn and pain;
In Thy service pain is pleasure;
With Thy favor loss is gain.
I have called Thee Abba, Father,
I have set my heart on Thee;
Storms may howl, and clouds may gather—
All must work for good to me.—Cho.

* *This Chorus may be used or omitted, according to circumstances.*

32.—GATHER THE CHILDREN.

Words by Rev. J. H. Martin. V. T. Barnwell.

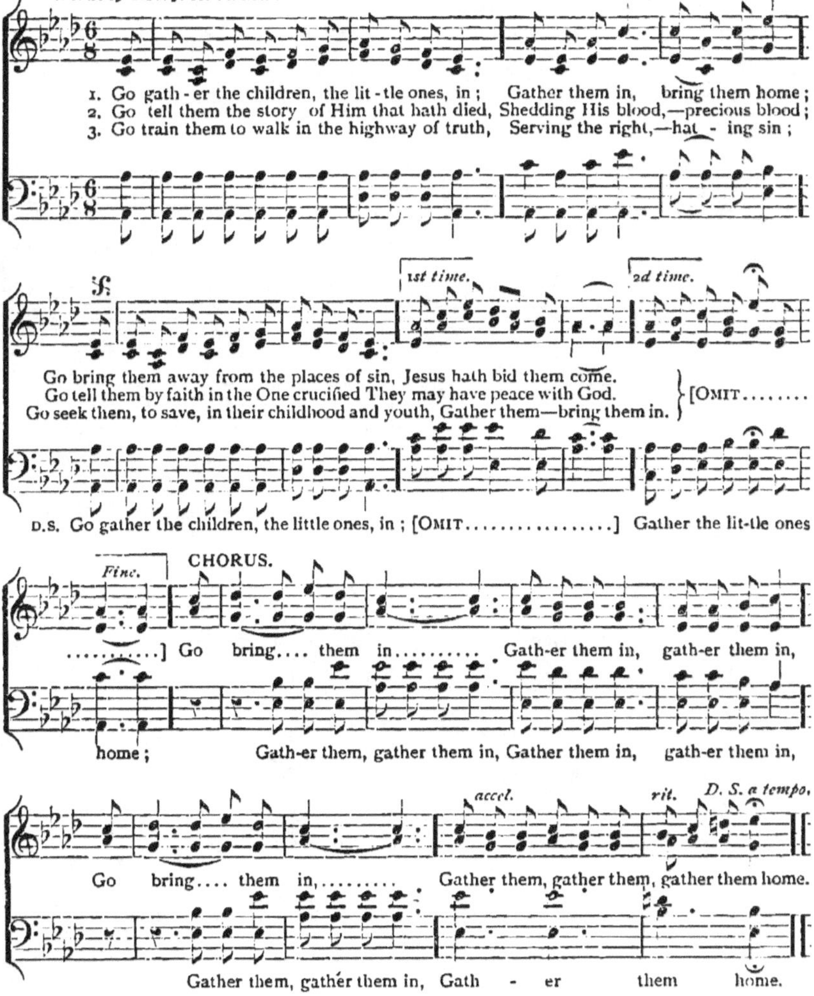
1. Go gath - er the children, the lit - tle ones, in ; Gather them in, bring them home ;
2. Go tell them the story of Him that hath died, Shedding His blood,—precious blood ;
3. Go train them to walk in the highway of truth, Serving the right,—hat - ing sin ;
1st time.
2d time.
Go bring them away from the places of sin, Jesus hath bid them come.
Go tell them by faith in the One crucified They may have peace with God.
Go seek them, to save, in their childhood and youth, Gather them—bring them in.
[Omit........
D.S. Go gather the children, the little ones, in ; [Omit..................] Gather the lit-tle ones
Fine.
CHORUS.
............] Go bring.... them in.......... Gath-er them in, gath-er them in,
home ; Gath-er them, gather them in, Gather them in, gath-er them in,
accel.
rit.
D. S. a tempo.
Go bring.... them in,......... Gather them, gather them, gather them home.
Gather them, gather them in, Gath - er them home.

33.—OLIPHANT. 8s, 7s & 4s.

WM. WILLIAMS. L. MASON. *From the German.*

1. Guide me, O Thou great Jehovah, Pilgrim thro' this barren land; I am weak, but Thou art mighty; Hold me with Thy powerful hand: Bread of heaven, Bread of heaven, Feed me till I want no more, Feed me till I want no more.

2 Open, Lord, the crystal fountain
   Whence the healing waters flow;
Let the fiery, cloudy pillar,
   Lead me all my journey through:
      Strong Deliv'rer!
Be Thou still my strength and shield.

3 When I tread the verge of Jordan,
   Bid my anxious fears subside:
Death of death, and hell's destruction,
   Land me safe on Canaan's side:
      Songs of praises
I will ever give to Thee.

34.—8s, 7s & 4s.

1 MIGHTY Lord, extend Thine empire!
   Be Thy truth with triumph crowned!
Let the lands that sit in darkness
   Hear the glorious gospel's sound,
      From our borders,
To the world's remotest bound.

2 By Thine arm, eternal Father,
   Scatter far the shades of night!
Let the great Immanuel's kingdom
   Open like the morning light,
      And the future
Realize our visions bright.

3 Come, too long to earth a stranger,
   Once again thy reign restore!
In Thy strength, ride forth and conquer,
   Still advancing more and more,
      Till the heathen
Shall the Lord supreme adore.
              Joseph Cottle.

35.—EVEN ME. 8s, 7s & 3s.

ELIZABETH CODNER.   W. B. BRADBURY.*

1. Lord, I hear of showers of bless-ing, Thou art scattering full and free;
Showers, the thirst-y land re-fresh-ing; Let some droppings fall on me.
E-ven me, E-ven me, Let some drop-pings fall on me.

2 Pass me not, O gracious Father,
   Sinful though my heart may be ;
   Thou might'st leave me, but the rather
   Let Thy mercy light on me,
      Even me.

3 Pass me not, O tender Saviour;
   Let me love and cling to Thee ;
   I am longing for Thy favor;
   When Thou comest, call for me,
      Even me.

4 Pass not, O mighty Spirit ;
   Thou canst make the blind to see ;
   Witnesser of Jesus' merit,
   Speak the word of power to me,
      Even me.

5 Have I long in sin been sleeping ?
   Long been slighting, grieving Thee ?
   Has the world my heart been keeping ?
   Oh, forgive and rescue me,
      Even me.

36.—TO-DAY.

L. MASON.

1 TO-DAY the Saviour calls:
   Ye wand'rers, come :
   Oh, ye benighted souls,
   Why longer roam ?

2 To-day the Saviour calls :
   For refuge fly ;
   The storm of vengeance falls,
   Ruin is nigh.

3 To-day the Saviour calls :
   Oh, listen now :
   Within these sacred walls
   To Jesus bow.

4 The Spirit calls to-day ;
   Yield to His power ;
   Oh, grieve Him not away,
   'Tis mercy's hour.

* *From "Golden Shower," by permission of Biglow & Main.*

37.—SICILY. 8s, 7s & 4s.

THOMAS KELLY.   *Italian.*

1. In Thy name, O Lord, as-sembling, We, Thy peo-ple, now draw near;
{ Teach us to re-joice with trembling; Speak, and let Thy servants hear; }
{ Hear with meekness, Hear with meeknsss, Hear Thy word with god-ly fear. }

2 While our days on earth are lengthened,
   May we give them, Lord, to Thee;
Cheered by hope, and daily strengthened,
   We would run, nor weary be,
      Till Thy glory,
Without clouds, in heaven we see.

3 There, in worship purer, sweeter,
   All Thy people shall adore,
Tasting of enjoyment greater
   Than they could conceive before,—
      Full enjoyment,—
Full, unmixed, and evermore.

38.—TAMWORTH. 8s, 7s & 4s.

LOCKHART.

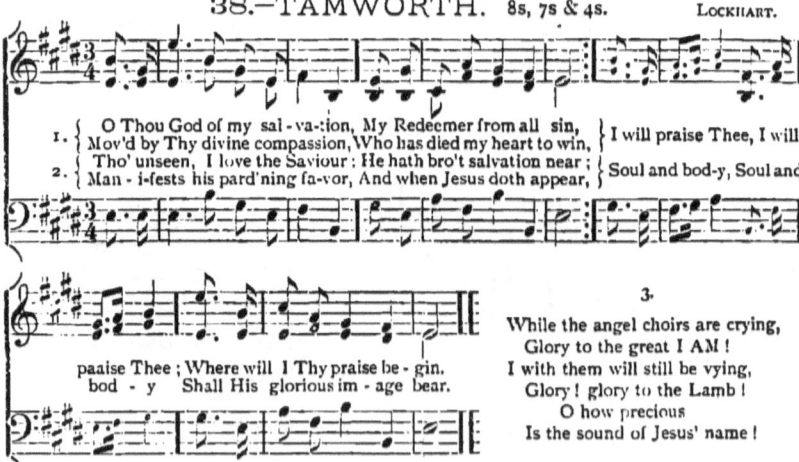

1. { O Thou God of my sal-va-tion, My Redeemer from all sin, } { I will praise Thee, I will
   { Mov'd by Thy divine compassion, Who has died my heart to win, }
2. { Tho' unseen, I love the Saviour; He hath bro't salvation near; } { Soul and bod-y, Soul and
   { Man-i-fests his pard'ning fa-vor, And when Jesus doth appear; }

paaise Thee; Where will I Thy praise be-gin.
bod-y Shall His glorious im-age bear.

3.
While the angel choirs are crying,
Glory to the great I AM!
I with them will still be vying,
Glory! glory to the Lamb!
   O how precious
Is the sound of Jesus' name!

39.—WATCHMAN, TELL US OF THE NIGHT.

With Deliberation. L. Mason.

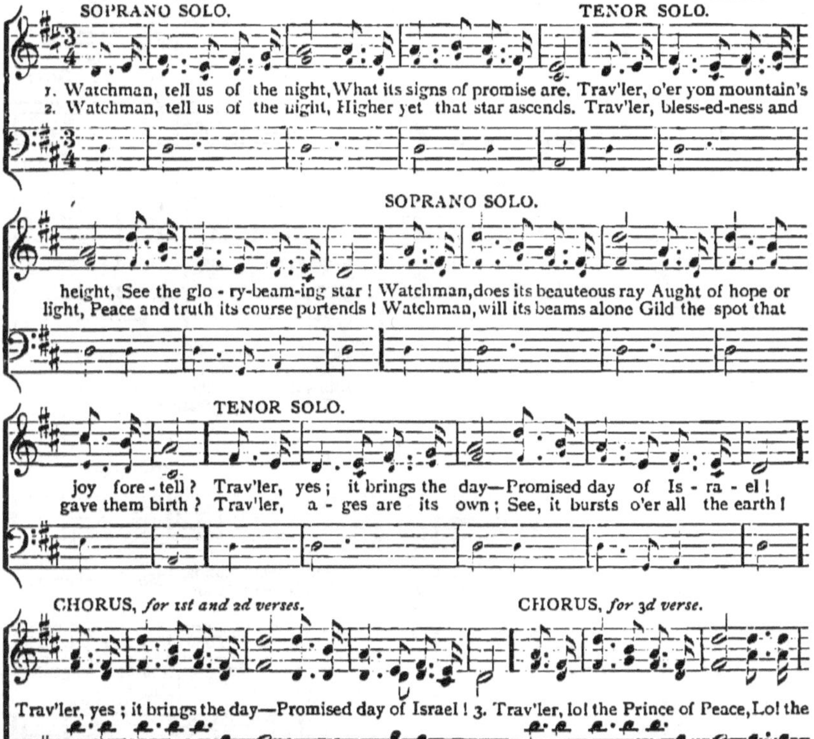
SOPRANO SOLO.
TENOR SOLO.
1. Watchman, tell us of the night, What its signs of promise are. Trav'ler, o'er yon mountain's
2. Watchman, tell us of the night, Higher yet that star ascends. Trav'ler, bless-ed-ness and
SOPRANO SOLO.
height, See the glo - ry-beam-ing star! Watchman, does its beauteous ray Aught of hope or
light, Peace and truth its course portends! Watchman, will its beams alone Gild the spot that
TENOR SOLO.
joy fore - tell? Trav'ler, yes; it brings the day—Promised day of Is - ra - el!
gave them birth? Trav'ler, a - ges are its own; See, it bursts o'er all the earth!
CHORUS, *for 1st and 2d verses.*
CHORUS, *for 3d verse.*
Trav'ler, yes; it brings the day—Promised day of Israel! 3. Trav'ler, lo! the Prince of Peace, Lo! the

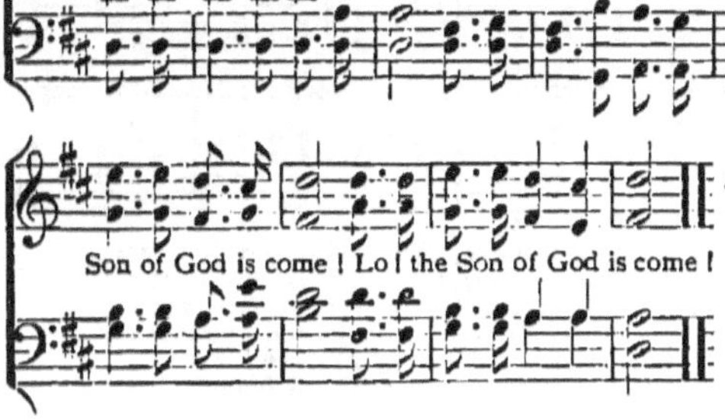
Son of God is come! Lo! the Son of God is come!

3 Watchman, tell us of the night,
For the morning seems to dawn.
Trav'ler, darkness takes its flight,
Doubt and terror are withdrawn!
Watchman, let thy wanderings cease;
Hie thee to thy quiet home.
Trav'ler, lo! the Prince of Peace—
Lo! the Son of God is come!

2 On the Rock of Ages founded;
  What can shake thy sure repose?
  With salvation's walls surrounded,
  Thou mayst smile on all thy foes.

3 See, the streams of living waters,
  Springing from eternal love,
  Still supply thy sons and daughters,
  And all fear of want remove.

2 Has thy night been long and mournful?
  Have thy friends unfaithful proved?
  Have thy foes been proud and scornful,
  By thy sighs and tears unmoved?
    Cease thy mourning:
  Zion still is well beloved.

3 God, thy God, will now restore thee:
  He Himself appears thy Friend;
  All thy foes shall flee before thee:
  Here their boasts and triumphs end:
    Great deliverance
  Zion's King will surely send.

3 When on Calvary I rest,
God, in flesh made manifest,
Shines in my Redeemer's face,
Full of beauty, truth, and grace.

4 Here I would forever stay,
Weep and gaze my soul away;
Thou art heaven on earth to me,
Lovely, mournful Calvary.

45.—THE BLESSED MERCY-SEAT.

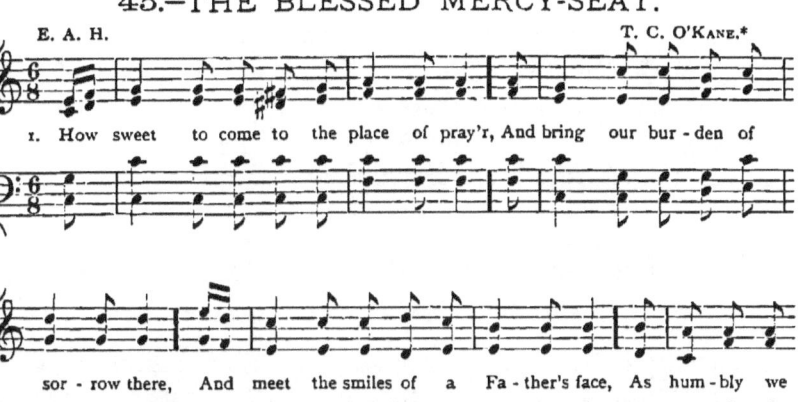

2 How sweet to come to the place of prayer,
   And lay our humble petitions there,
   Assured the Father will hear our plea,
   And pour in our spirits His love so free.—Cho.

3 How sweet to come to the place of prayer,
   And feast our souls in communion there;
   And feel the rapture that thrills our hearts,
   As Jesus His quickening love imparts.—Cho.

*From "Songs of Faith," by per. S. Brainard's Sons.

48.—THE KINGDOM COMING.

M. B. C. Slade.  R. M. McIntosh, *by per*.

1. From all the dark places Of earth's heathen races, Oh, see how the dark shadows fly!
The voice of sal-va-tion A-wakes ev-ery na-tion, Come o-ver and help us, they cry.

CHORUS.

The king-dom is com-ing, Oh, tell ye the sto-ry, God's banner ex-alt-ed shall be!
The earth shall be full of His knowledge and glory, As wa-ters that cov-er the sea!

2 The sunlight is glancing
O'er armies advancing,
To conquer the kingdoms of sin;
Our Lord shall possess them,
His presence shall bless them,
His beauty shall enter them in.—Cho.

3 With shouting and singing,
And jubilant ringing,
Their arms of rebellion cast down;
At last every nation,
The Lord of salvation,
Their King and Redeemer shall own.—Cho.

2 Other refuge have I none;
   Hangs my helpless soul on Thee:
Leave, O leave me not alone,
   Still support and comfort me:
All my trust on Thee is stayed,
   All my help from Thee I bring;
Cover my defenseless head
   With the shadow of Thy wing!

3 Thou, O Christ, art all I want;
   More than all in Thee I find;
Raise the fallen, cheer the faint,
   Heal the sick, and lead the blind.
Just and holy is Thy name,
   I am all unrighteousness:
False and full of sin I am,
   Thou art full of truth and grace.

50.—PASS ME NOT. 8s & 5s.

Fanny Crosby Van Alstyne. W. H. Doane.*

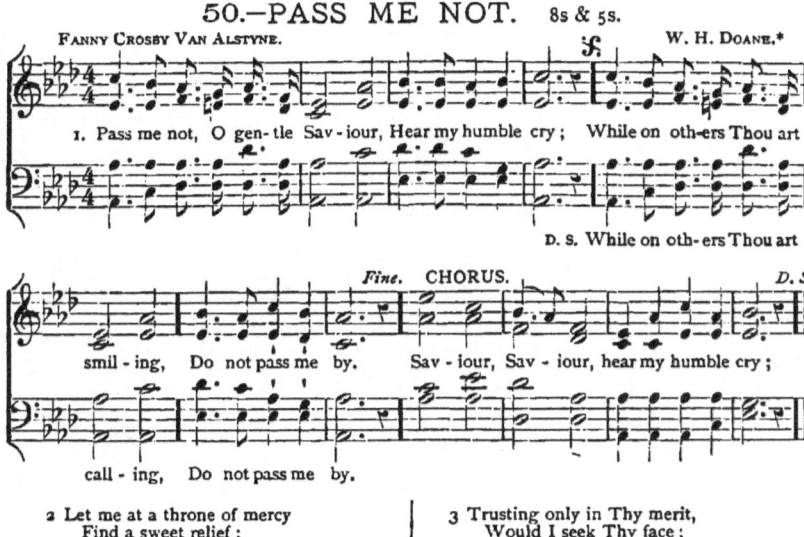

1. Pass me not, O gen-tle Sav-iour, Hear my humble cry; While on oth-ers Thou art smil-ing, Do not pass me by. Sav-iour, Sav-iour, hear my humble cry; While on oth-ers Thou art call-ing, Do not pass me by.

2 Let me at a throne of mercy
   Find a sweet relief;
   Kneeling there in deep contrition,
   Help my unbelief.—Cho.

3 Trusting only in Thy merit,
   Would I seek Thy face;
   Hear my wounded, broken spirit,
   Save me by Thy grace.—Cho.

51.—MARTYN. 7s. Double.

Simeon Butler Marsh.

* From "Pure Gold," by per. Biglow & Main.

54.—COLQUITT.

MALE VOICES.

Composed and Sung at International Sunday School Convention, Atlanta, Ga., April 17-19, 1878.

Thomas Raffles.   Wm. G. Fischer, *of Phila. By per.*

1. High in yon-der realms of light, Dwell the raptured saints a-bove; Far beyond our fee-ble sight, Hap-py in Im-manuel's love: Pilgrims in this vale of tears, Once they knew, like us be-low, Gloomy doubts, distressing fears, Torturing pain, and heavy woe.

2.
But these days of weeping o'er,
  Passed this scene of toil and pain,
They shall feel distress no more,
  Never, never weep again:
'Mid the chorus of the skies,
  'Mid th' angelic lyres above,
Hark, their songs melodious rise,
  Songs of praise to Jesus's love.

3.
All is tranquil and serene,
  Calm and undisturbed repose:
There no cloud can intervene,
  There no angry tempest blows:
Every tear is wiped away,
  Sighs no more shall heave the breast,
Night is lost in endless day,
  Sorrow, in eternal rest.

2 While we seek supplies of grace,
   Through the dear Redeemer's name,
Show Thy reconciling face,—
   Take away our sin and shame;
From our worldly cares set free,
May we rest this day in Thee.

3 Here we come Thy name to praise;
   Let us feel Thy presence near;
May Thy glory meet our eyes,
   While we in Thy house appear
Here afford us, Lord, a taste
Of our everlasting rest.

56.—SAVED EVERY MOMENT.

E. A. H. Mrs. Jos. F. Knapp.*

1. O the wondrous, wondrous power Of the precious blood divine, Washing, healing, cleansing, sealing This unworthy heart, unworthy heart of mine.
2. When I came to Christ for cleansing, My poor heart was all depraved; Now, O wonderful redemption, I am so completely, so completely saved!

CHORUS.
Ev-ery moment, every moment, I am saved by blood divine, Glo-ry, glo-ry be to Je-sus, I am His and He is mine; Glo-ry, glo-ry be to Je-sus! I am His and He is mine.

3 O the peace that comes from cleansing!
O the sweet and perfect rest!
O the joy beyond expressing!
I am so completely, so completely blest!

4 Glory, glory be to Jesus,
Who redeemed my helpless soul!
Glory, glory be to Jesus,
Who by cleansing makes me whole, yes, makes me whole!

* From "*Songs of Faith*," by permission of S. Brainard's Sons.

57.—SOLITUDE. 7s.   L. T. Downs.

1. Jesus, seek Thy wand'ring sheep;
Bring me back and lead and keep;
Take on Thee my ev'ry care;
Bear me, on Thy bosom bear.

2. Let me know my Shepherd's voice;
More and more in Thee rejoice;
More and more of Thee receive;
Ever in Thy Spirit live.

Chas. Wesley.

58.—TRINITY. 7s.   *English.*
CHORUS.

1. Depth of mercy! can there be
Mercy still reserved for me?
Can my God His wrath forbear?
Me, the chief of sinners, spare?
God is love, I know, I feel;
Jesus weeps and loves me still;
Jesus weeps, He weeps and loves me still.

2 I have long withstood His grace,
Long provoked Him to His face;
Would not hearken to His calls;
Grieved Him by a thousand falls.

3 Lo! I cumber still the ground;
Lo! an Advocate is found!
"Hasten not to cut him down;
Let this barren soul alone!"

4 Kindled His relentings are;
Me He now delights to spare;
Cries, "How shall I give thee up?"
Lets the lifted thunder drop.

5 There for me the Saviour stands;
Shows His wounds and spreads His hands;
God is love! I know, I feel;
Jesus weeps, and loves me still.

59.—PRAISE THE LORD!

Mrs. M. B. C. Slade.　　　　Dr. A. Brooks Everett.*

2 Love the Lord! love the Lord!
　Happy children, give Him your youth's
　　bright days;
　Love the Lord! love the Lord!
　He ever loveth you, He says.
　Oh, love Him, for He loves you so;
　Oh, love Him for His wondrous love;
　Love the Lord, here below,
　And love Him in His courts above.

3 Serve the Lord! serve the Lord!
　Happy children serve Him with songs
　　of joy;
　Serve the Lord! serve the Lord!
　And let His work your hands employ.
　Oh, serve Him, whatsoe'er ye do;
　Oh, serve Him, wheresoe'er ye move;
　Serve the Lord, here below,
　And serve Him in His courts above.

*By per. of R. M. McIntosh.

60.—BELTON. S. M.

Montgomery. / V. T. Barnwell.

1. Sow in the morn thy seed; At eve hold not thy hand;
To doubt and fear give thou no heed,— Broad-cast it o'er the land.

2 Thou know'st not which shall thrive,—
 The late or early sown;
 Grace keeps the precious germ alive
 When and wherever strown:

3 And duly shall appear,
 In verdure, beauty, strength,

The tender blade, the stalk, the ear,
 And the full corn at length.

4 Thou canst not toil in vain:
 Cold, heat, and moist, and dry,
 Shall foster and mature the grain
 For garners in the sky.

61.—BOYLSTON. S. M.

Chas. Wesley. / Dr. L. Mason.

1 Gracious Redeemer, shake
 This slumber from my soul!
 Say to me now, "Awake, awake!
 And Christ shall make thee whole."

2 Lay to Thy mighty hand;
 Alarm me in this hour;
 And make me fully understand
 The thunder of Thy power!

3 Give me on Thee to call,
 Always to watch and pray,
 Lest I into temptation fall,
 And cast my shield away.

4 For each assault prepared
 And ready may I be;
 For ever standing on my guard,
 And looking up to Thee.

62.—EVERY DAY AND HOUR.

FANNY J. CROSBY. W. H. DOANE.*

1. Sav-iour, more than life to me, I am clinging, clinging close to Thee;
Let Thy pre-cious blood ap-plied, Keep me ev-er, ev-er near Thy side.

REFRAIN.
Ev-ery day, ev-ery hour, Let me feel Thy cleansing
Ev-ery day and hour, Ev-ery day and hour,
power; May Thy ten-der love to me Bind me clos-er, clos-er, Lord, to Thee.

2 Through this changing world below,
Lead me gently, gently as I go;
Trusting Thee, I cannot stray,
I can never, never lose my way.
REF.—Every day and hour, etc.

3 Let me love Thee more and more,
Till this fleeting, fleeting life is o'er;
Till my soul is lost in love,
In a brighter, brighter world above.
REF.—Every day and hour, etc.

* From "Brightest and Best," by permission of Biglow & Main, N. Y.

63.—DENNIS. S. M.

BEDDOME. Arr. from NAGELI.

1. Come, Holy Spirit, come, With energy divine, And on this poor, benighted soul With beams of mercy shine.

2 Melt, melt this frozen heart;
   This stubborn will subdue;
   Each evil passion overcome,
   And form me all anew.

3 Mine will the profit be,
   But Thine shall be the praise;
   And unto Thee will I devote
   The remnant of my days.

64.—DOVER. S. M.

CHAS. WESLEY. English Tune.

1. Messiah, full of grace, Redeem'd by Thee, we plead The promise made to Abrah'm's race, To souls for ages dead.
2. Their bones, as quite dried up, Throughout the vale appear: Cut off and lost their last faint hope To see Thy kingdom here.

3 Open their graves, and bring
   The outcasts forth, to own
   Thou art their Lord, their God, their King,
   Their true Anointed One.

4 To save the race forlorn
   Thy glorious arm display!
   And show the world a nation born,
   A nation in a day!

65.—AFTER THE HARVEST, GOLDEN SHEAVES.

Mrs. Mary E. Kail.   J. R. Murray.*

1. After the harvest, golden sheaves; And when the harvester's work is done,
Joy, and glory, and perfect peace— In the new life begun.

REFRAIN.
This shall the song of the reaper be, Rest, at closing of day, for me;
Then, on the blessed Redeemer's breast, I shall lie down to blissful rest.

2 After the harvest, golden sheaves;
  Gathered around at the Master's feet,
'Mid sweet songs of triumphant praise,
  Making our joy complete.—Ref.

3 After the harvest, golden sheaves;
  Then let us work while the days are long,
When the Lord of the harvest comes,
  Join in the reaper's song.—Ref.

* From "*Heavenward*," by per. S. Brainard's Sons.

71.—MARCHING HOME.

FRANK M. DAVIS.*

2 In that blessed land we're nearing now,
  We shall see our Saviour's face;
  He will place a crown on every brow,
  Saved by His redeeming grace.—CHO.

3 Brothers, will you join our happy band,
  Traveling up the shining way?
  Jesus is the Captain in command:
  Will you now His call obey?—CHO.

* From the "Pearl," by per. S. Brainard's Sons.

3 Along its shore, angelic bands
    Watch every moving wave;
    With holy joy their breast expands,
    When men the waters crave.—Cho.

4 To it distressed souls repair,
    The Lord invites them nigh;
    They leave their cares and sorrows there,—
    They drink and never die.—Cho.

* *From the "Welcome," by permission of S. Brainard's Sons.*

75.—OLNEY. S. M.

H. U. Onderdonk.   Dr. L. Mason.

1. The Spir-it, in our hearts, Is whisp'ring, "Sin-ner, come;" The bride, the church of Christ, proclaims To all His children, "Come!"
2. Let him that hear-eth say To all a-bout him, "Come;" Let him that thirsts for right-eous-ness To Christ, the fountain, come.

3 Yes, whosoever will,
   Oh, let him freely come,
And freely drink the stream of life;
   'Tis Jesus bids him come.

4 Lo! Jesus, who invites,
   Declares, "I quickly come;"
Lord, even so; we wait Thy hour;
   O blest Redeemer, come.

76.—OZREM. S. M.

Benj. Beddome.   I. B. Woodbury.

1. Did Christ o'er sin-ners weep, And shall our cheeks be dry? Let floods of pen-i-tential grief Burst forth from ev-ery eye.

2 The Son of God in tears
   The wondering angels see!
Be thou astonished, O my soul;
   He shed those tears for thee.

3 He wept that we might weep;
   Each sin demands a tear;
In heaven alone no sin is found,
   And there's no weeping there.

77.—THE GATE AJAR.

S. J. Vail.*

1. There is a gate that stands a-jar, And thro' its por-tal gleam-ing, A ra-diance from the Cross a-far The Sav-iour's love re-veal-ing.

REFRAIN.
Oh! depths of mer-cy! can it be That gate was left a-jar for me? For me, for me, Was left a-jar for me.... For me, for me?

2 That gate ajar stands free for all
  Who seek through it salvation ;
 The rich, and poor, the great and small,
  Of every tribe and nation.—Ref.

3 Press onward, then, though foes may frown,
  While mercy's gate is open,
  Accept the cross, and win the crown,
  Love's everlasting token.—Ref.

4 Beyond the river's brink we'll lay
  The cross that here is given ;
  And bear the crown of life away,
  And love Him more in heaven.—Ref.

* From "Song Sermons," by per. of Philip Phillips.

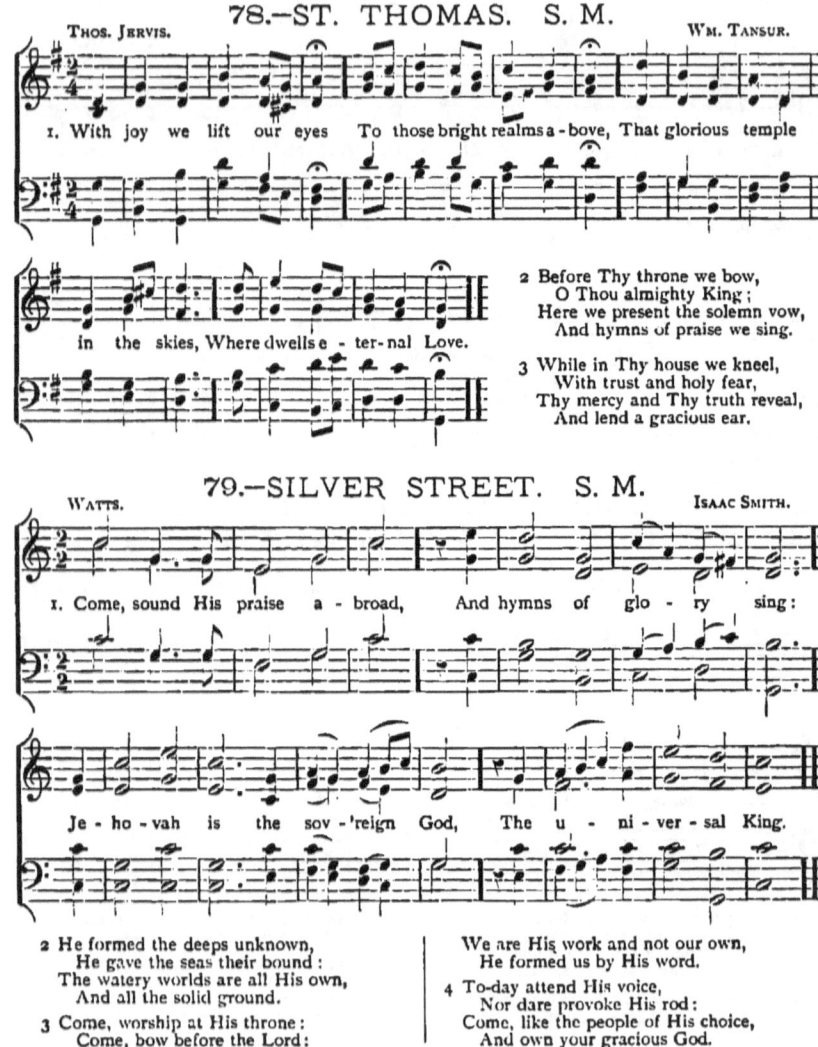

80.—WHAT MUST IT BE TO BE THERE!

J. M. KIEFFER.*

1. We talk of the realms of the bless'd,
   That country so bright and so fair,
   And oft are its glo-ries confess'd,
   But what must it be to be there!

2. We talk of its pathways of gold,
   Its walls decked with jewels so rare;
   Its won-ders and pleasures un-told,
   But what must it be to be there!

CHORUS

Oh, what must it be to be there!...... Oh, what must it be to be there!
With Je-sus, our friend, All e-ter-ni-ty to spend, Oh, what must it be to be there.

3 We talk of its freedom from sin,
   From sorrow, temptation and care,
   From trials without and within;
   But what must it be to be there!—CHO.

4 We talk of its peace and its love,
   The robes which the glorified wear;
   The songs of the blessed above,
   But what must it be to be there!—CHO.

* From the "Pearl," by per. S. Brainard's Sons.

2 Waiting there with smiling faces,
  In their spotless robes of white;
  While far out upon the billows
  Comes to us a gleam of light.

3 But we soon shall pass the portal,
  Then we'll grasp the kindly hand;
  Soon we'll greet the forms that bind us
  To the blessed glory-land.

* From "*Joyful Songs*," by permission of S. Brainard's Sons.

84.—DUKE STREET. L. M.

J. Hatton.

1. Je-ho-vah reigns; His throne is high; His robes are light and maj-es-ty; His glo-ry shines with beams so bright, No mortal can sus-tain the sight.

2 His terrors keep the world in awe;
His justice guards His holy law;
His love reveals a smiling face;
His truth and promise seal the grace.

3 Through all His works His wisdom shines,
And baffles Satan's deep designs;
His power is sovereign to fulfil
The noblest counsels of His will.

85.—EFFINGHAM. L. M.

Watts. *English.*

1. Great God, in-dulge my hum-ble claim, Be Thou my hope, my joy, my rest; The glo-ries that com-pose Thy name Stand all engaged to make me blest.

2 Thou great and good, Thou just and wise,
Thou art my Father and my God;
And I am Thine by sacred ties,—
Thy son, Thy servant bought with blood.

3 I'll lift my hands, I'll raise my voice,
While I have breath to pray or praise:
This work shall make my heart rejoice,
And fill the remnant of my days.

V. T. Barnwell.

1. Af-flic-tions though they seem se-vere, In mer-cy oft are sent,
They stopped the prod-i-gal's ca-reer, And caused him to re-pent.

CHORUS.
I'll not die here for bread, he cries, Nor starve in for-eign lands;
My fa-ther's house hath large sup-plies, And bounteous are his hands.

2 What have I gained by sin, he said,
But hunger, shame, and fear :
My father's house abounds in bread,
While I am starving here.—Cho.

3 I'll go and tell him all I've done,
Fall down before his face,
Unworthy to be called his son,
I'll seek a servant's place.—Cho.

4 His father saw him coming back,
He saw, he ran, he smiled ;
And threw his arms around the neck
Of his rebellious child.—Cho.

5 O father, I have sinned, forgive—
Enough, the father said :
Rejoice, my house, my son 's alive,
For whom I mourned as dead.—Cho.

87.—FEDERAL STREET. L. M.

DODDRIDGE.   H. K. OLIVER.

1. My gracious Lord, I own Thy right
To ev-ery ser-vice I can pay,
And call it my su-preme de-light
To hear Thy dic-tates and o-bey.

2 What is my being but for Thee,
  Its sure support, its noblest end?
'Tis my delight Thy face to see,
  And serve the cause of such a friend.

3 'Tis to my Saviour I would live,
  To Him who for my ransom died;
Nor could all worldly honour give
  Such bliss as crowns me at His side.

88.—FOREST. L. M.

WATTS.   CHAPIN.

1. When I sur-vey the wondrous cross
On which the Prince of glo-ry died,
My richest gain I count but loss,
And pour contempt on all my pride.

2 See, from His head, His hands, His feet,
  Sorrow and love flow mingled down:
Did e'er such love and sorrow meet,
  Or thorns compose so rich a crown?

3 Were the whole realm of nature mine
  That were a present far too small;
Love so amazing, so divine,
  Demands my soul, my life, my all.

89.—THE RIVER OF SONG.

Fanny Crosby.   W. H. Doane.*

1. O the sleep of just a moment, When the spirit sinks away! Then the waking, blissful waking, In a world of endless day!
2. We shall hear celestial music O'er its bosom sweep along, Like the voice of many waters; Hark! the everlasting song.

CHORUS.
O the rapture, holy rapture, There to stand with the bright, happy throng! There the sacred springs of pleasure With the streams of love unite, In a pure, flowing river of song.

3 In their numbers far excelling
  All the countless orbs above,
They who swell the mighty chorus,
  In the spirit world of love.—Cho.

4 Worthy is the Lamb forever,
  Worthy is the Lamb, they cry;
Glory, glory, hallelujah,
  Glory be to God most high!—Cho.

* From "Royal Diadem," by per. Biglow & Main, N. Y.

92.—AROUND THE THRONE.

Anon.

1. A-round the throne of God in heaven, Thousands of chil-dren stand;
Chil-dren, whose sins are all for-giv'n, A ho-ly, hap-py band,
Sing-ing, Glo-ry, glo-ry, glo-ry be to God on high.

2.
In flowing robes of spotless white
See every one arrayed;
Dwelling in everlasting light,
And joys that never fade,
  Singing, Glory, glory, etc.

3.
What brought them to that world above—
That heaven so bright and fair,
Where all is peace and joy and love?
How came those children there?
  Singing, Glory, glory, etc.

4.
Because the Saviour shed His blood
To wash away their sin:
Bathed in that pure and precious flood,
Behold them white and clean,
  Singing, Glory, glory, etc.

5.
On earth they sought the Saviour's grace,
On earth they loved His name;
So now they see His blessed face,
And stand before the Lamb,
  Singing, Glory, glory, etc.

93.—MENDON. L. M.

COLLYER.   German.

1. As-sem-bled at Thy great command, Be-fore Thy face, dread King, we stand:
The voice that marshaled ev-ery star Has called Thy peo-ple from a-far.

2 We meet, through distant lands to spread
The truth for which the martyrs bled;
Along the line, to either pole,
The anthem of Thy praise to roll.

3 Our prayers assist; accept our praise;
Our hopes revive; our courage raise;
Our counsels aid; to each impart
The single eye, the faithful heart.

94.—MISSIONARY CHANT.

KELLY.   CHARLES ZEUNER.

1. O where is now that glowing love That mark'd our u-nion with the Lord?
Our hearts were fixed on things a-bove, Nor could the world a joy af-ford.

2 Where are the happy seasons, spent
In fellowship with Him we loved?
The sacred joy, the sweet content,
The blessedness that then we proved?

3 Behold, again we turn to Thee;
O cast us not away, though vile:
No peace we have, no joy we see,
O Lord our God, but in Thy smile.

95.—HOME, SWEET HOME!

DENHAM.
SIR HENRY ROWLEY BISHOP.

1. 'Mid scenes of con-fu-sion and crea-ture complaints, How sweet to the soul is com-mu-nion with saints! To find at the ban-quet of mer-cy there's room, And feel in the pres-ence of Je-sus at home. Home! home! sweet, sweet home! Pre-pare me, dear Sav-iour, for glo-ry, my home.

2 Sweet bonds that unite all the children of peace !
And thrice precious Jesus, whose love cannot cease !
Though oft from Thy presence in sadness I roam,
I long to behold Thee in glory, at home.

3 I sigh from this body of sin to be free,
Which hinders my joy and communion with Thee :
Though now my temptation like billows may foam,
All, all will be peace, when I'm with Thee at home.

96.—ORLAND. L. M.
Watts. — Dr. Arnold.

1. Jesus shall reign where'er the sun Doth his suc-cess-ive jour-neys run; His kingdom spread from shore to shore, Till moons shall wax and wane no more.

2 From north to south the princes meet
To pay their homage at His feet;
While western empires own their Lord,
And savage tribes attend His word.

3 To Him shall endless prayer be made,
And endless praises crown His head;
His Name, like sweet perfume, shall rise
With every morning sacrifice.

97.—OLD HUNDRED. L. M.
Mant. — G. Franc.

1. Hear ye my law, my peo-ple, hear; Lend to my words a list'-ning ear;
My mouth shall loft-y lore un-fold, My lips dark sen-ten-ces of old.

2. His law to Ja-cob He revealed, His cov-e-nant with Is-rael sealed;
And gave our sires the charge di-vine, In trust for their suc-ceed-ing line.—

3 That year to year, and age to age,
Might safe convey the sacred page;
And still His truth perpetual run,
Transmitted down from sire to son;

4 That on the arm of power divine,
Sons yet unborn might still recline;
Nor e'er forget the works of God,
Nor e'er forsake His guiding rod.

98.—LOVING-KINDNESS. L. M.

Samuel Medley.   *Western Melody.*

1. A-wake, my soul, in joy-ful lays, And sing thy great Redeemer's praise;
He just-ly claims a song from me. His lov-ing-kind-ness is so free!
His lov-ing-kind-ness, lov-ing-kind-ness, His lov-ing-kind-ness is so free!

2 He saw me ruined in the fall,
Yet loved me notwithstanding all;
He saved me from my lost estate,
His loving-kindness is so great.

3 Through mighty hosts of cruel foes,
Where earth and hell my way oppose,
He safely leads my soul along,
His loving-kindness is so strong.

4 Often I feel my sinful heart
Prone from Jesus to depart;
And though I oft have Him forgot,
His loving-kindness changes not.

5 So when I pass death's gloomy vale,
And life and mortal powers shall fail,
O, may my last expiring breath
His loving-kindness sing in death!

6 Then shall I mount and soar away
To the bright world of endless day;
Then shall I sing with sweet surprise
His loving-kindness in the skies!

3 We, too, shall come to the river-side,
    Gathering one by one ;
  Nearer its waters each eventide,
    Gathering one by one ;
  O Jesus, our fainting strength uphold,
  The waves of that river are dark and cold ;
  Gathering homeward from every land,
    Gathering one by one.—REF.

4 Jesus, Redeemer, be Thou our stay !
    Gathering one by one ;
  Cross the dark river with us, we pray,
    Gathering one by one ;
  Then boldly we'll come to Jordan's side,
  And fearlessly breast its swelling tide,
  Gathering homeward from every land,
    Gathering one by one.—REF.

103.—PROTECTION. 11s.

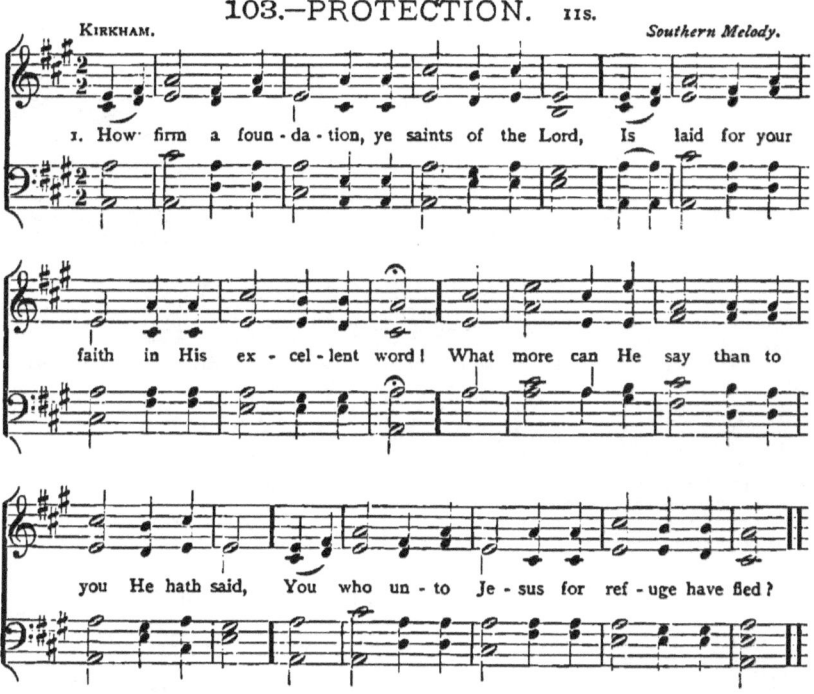

Kirkham. Southern Melody.

1. How firm a foun-da-tion, ye saints of the Lord, Is laid for your faith in His ex-cel-lent word! What more can He say than to you He hath said, You who un-to Je-sus for ref-uge have fled?

2 In every condition—in sickness, in health;
In poverty's vale, or abounding in wealth;
At home and abroad; on the land, on the sea—
"As thy days may demand, shall thy strength ever be.

3 "Fear not; I am with thee; O be not dismayed!
I, I am thy God, and will still give thee aid;
I'll strengthen thee, help thee, and cause thee to stand,
Upheld by My righteous, omnipotent hand.

4 "When through the deep waters I call thee to go,
The rivers of woe shall not thee overflow;
For I will be with thee, thy troubles to bless,
And sanctify to thee thy deepest distress.

5 "When through fiery trials thy pathway shall lie,
My grace, all-sufficient, shall be thy supply:
The flame shall not hurt thee ;—I only design
Thy dross to consume, and thy gold to refine.

6 "E'en down to old age, all my people shall prove
My sovereign, eternal, unchangeable love;
And when hoary hairs shall their temples adorn,
Like lambs they shall still in my bosom be borne.

7 "The soul that on Jesus still leans for repose,
I *will* not, I *will* not desert to his foes;
That soul, though all hell should endeavor to shake,
I'll never, *no, never*, NO, NEVER forsake."

104.—REST. L. M.

DODDRIDGE. W. B. BRADBURY.

1. A-rise, my tend'rest thoughts, a-rise; To tor-rents melt my streaming eyes;
And thou, my heart, with an-guish feel Those e-vils which thou canst not heal.

2 My God, I feel the mournful scene :
My bowels yearn o'er dying men ;
And fain my pity would reclaim,
And snatch the firebrands from the flame.

3 But feeble my compassion proves,
And can but weep where most it loves ;
Thy own all-saving arm employ,
And turn these drops of grief to joy.

105.—ROCKINGHAM. L. M.

DR. L. MASON.

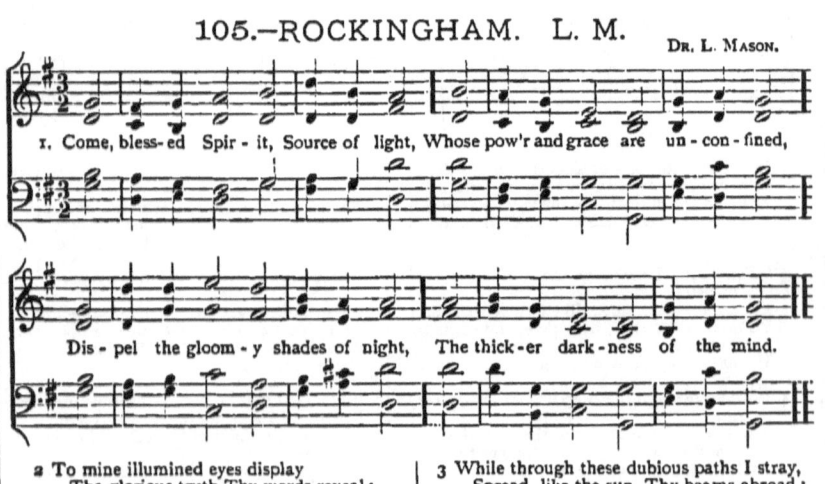

1. Come, bless-ed Spir-it, Source of light, Whose pow'r and grace are un-con-fined,
Dis-pel the gloom-y shades of night, The thick-er dark-ness of the mind.

2 To mine illumined eyes display
The glorious truth Thy words reveal ;
Cause me to run the heavenly way ;
Make me delight to do Thy will.

3 While through these dubious paths I stray,
Spread, like the sun, Thy beams abroad ;
Oh, show the dangers of the way,
And guide my feeble steps to God.

106.—ASSURANCE. C. M. D.

CHAS. WESLEY. Scotch Melody.

1. How happy every child of grace, Who knows his sins forgiven!
This earth, he cries, is not my place, I seek my place in heaven;
A country far from mortal sight; Yet, O! by faith I see
The land of rest, the saints' delight, The heaven prepared for me.

2 A stranger in the world below,
    I calmly sojourn here;
  Nor can its happiness or woe,
    Provoke my hope or fear;
  Its evils in a moment end,
    Its joys as soon are past;
  But, O! the bliss to which I tend
    Eternally shall last.

3 To that Jerusalem above
    With singing I repair;
  While in the flesh, my hope and love,
    My heart and soul, are there.
  There my exalted Saviour stands
    My merciful High Priest,
  And still extends His wounded hands,
    To take me to His breast.

2 From heaven He came, of heaven He spoke,
  To heaven He led His followers' way;
  Dark clouds of gloomy night He broke,
  Unveiling an immortal day.

3 "Come, wand'rers, to my Father's home;
  Come, all ye weary ones, and rest;"
  Yes, sacred Teacher, we will come,
  Obey Thee, love Thee, and be blest.

2 "I'll make your great commission known;
  And ye shall prove my gospel true,
  By all the works that I have done,
  By all the wonders ye shall do.

3 "Teach all the nations my commands,
  I'm with you till the world shall end;
  All power is trusted in My hands,
  I can destroy, and I defend."

109.—AIN. S. M. D.

CHAS. WESLEY. CORELLI.

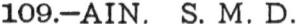

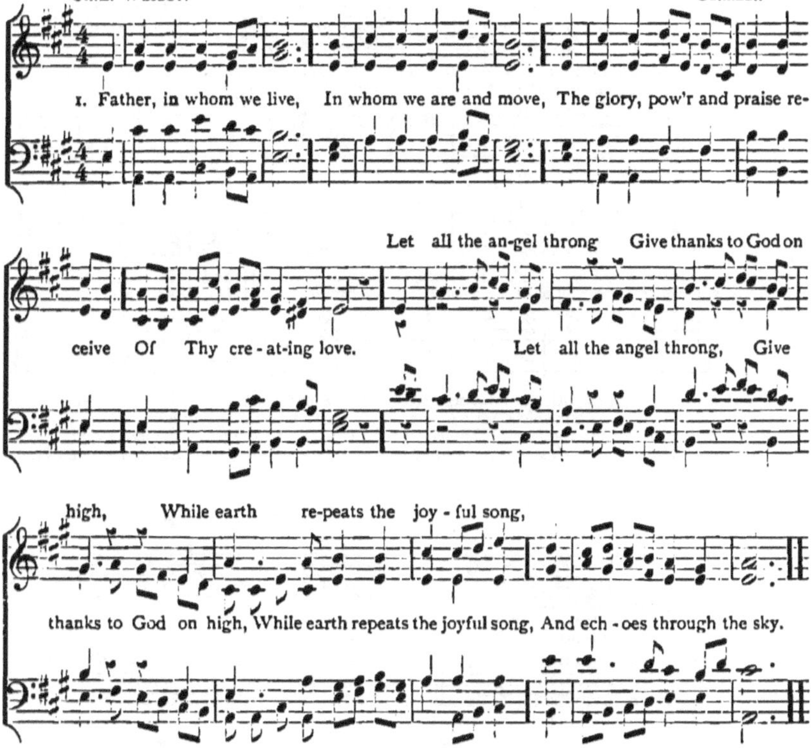
1. Father, in whom we live, In whom we are and move, The glory, pow'r and praise re-
Let all the an-gel throng Give thanks to God on
ceive Of Thy cre-at-ing love. Let all the angel throng, Give
high, While earth re-peats the joy-ful song,
thanks to God on high, While earth repeats the joyful song, And ech-oes through the sky.

2 Incarnate Deity,
Let all the ransomed race
Render, in thanks, their lives to Thee,
For Thy redeeming grace;
The grace to sinners showed,
Ye heavenly choirs proclaim,
And cry, "Salvation to our God,
Salvation to the Lamb!"

3 Spirit of holiness,
Let all Thy saints adore
Thy sacred energy, and bless
Thy heart-renewing power.
Not angel tongues can tell
Thy love's ecstatic height,
The glorious joy unspeakable,
The beatific sight!

4 Eternal, Triune Lord,
Let all the hosts above,
Let all the sons of men, record,
And dwell upon Thy love.
When heaven and earth are fled
Before Thy glorious face,
Sing all the saints Thy love hath made,
Thine everlasting praise!

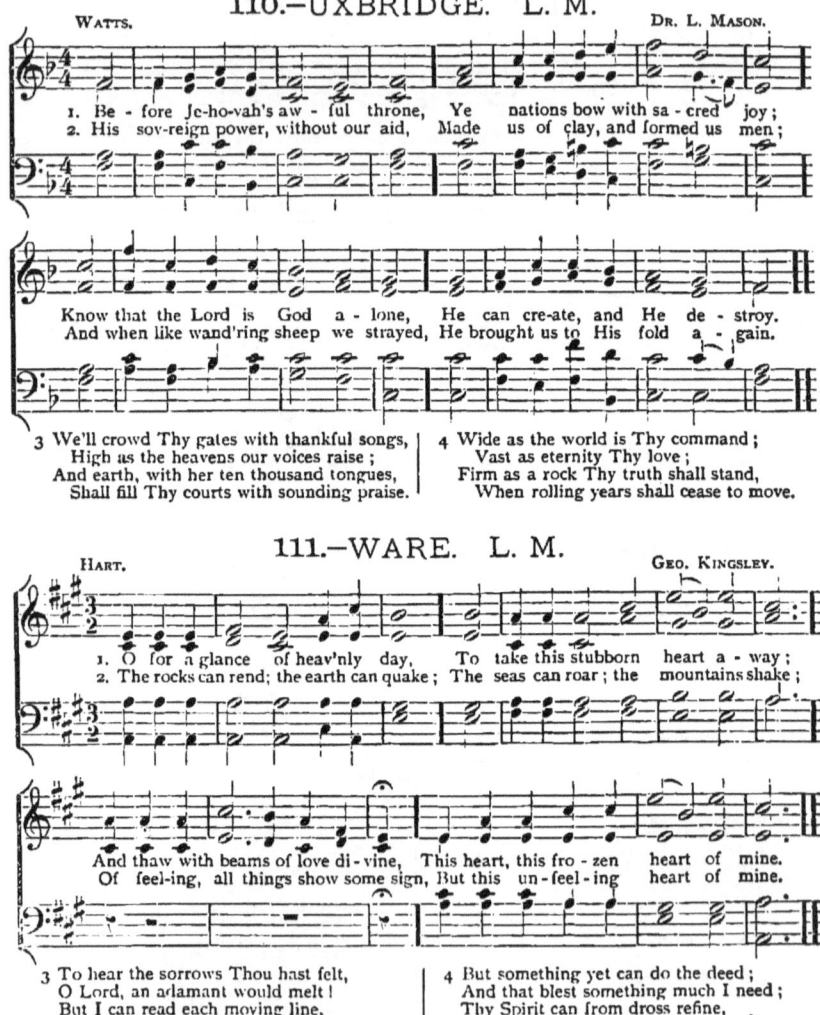

112.—IDDO. C. M. D.

NAGELI.

1. Oh, praise our great and gracious Lord, And call upon His name: To strains of joy tune every chord, His mighty acts proclaim. Tell how He led His chosen race To Canaan's promised land; Tell how His covenant of grace Unchanged shall ever stand, Unchanged shall ever stand.

2 We, too, have manna from above,—
The bread that came from heaven;
To us the same kind hand of love
Hath living waters given.
A rock we have, from whence the spring
In rich abundance flows;
That rock is Christ, our Priest, our King,
Who life and health bestows.

3 Oh, let us prize this blessed food,
And trust our heavenly Guide;
So shall we find death's fearful flood
Serene as Jordan's tide;
And safely reach that happy shore,
The land of peace and rest,
Where angels worship and adore,
In God's own presence bless'd.

113.—WELLS. L. M.

Watts.   Holdroyd.

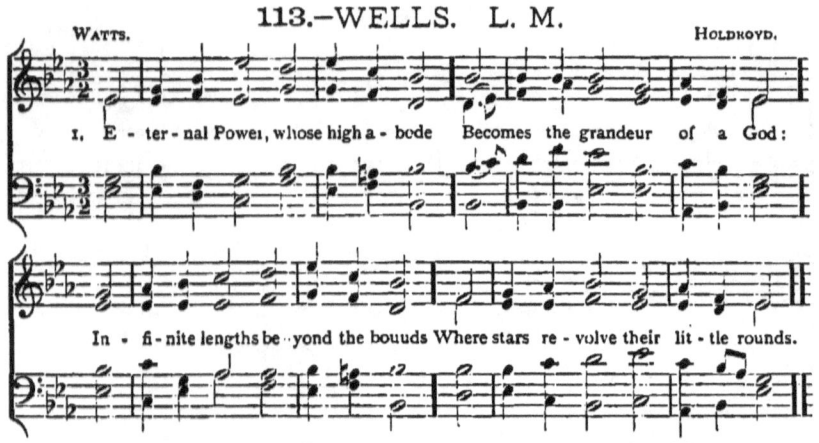

1. E - ter - nal Power, whose high a - bode Becomes the grandeur of a God:
In - fi - nite lengths beyond the bounds Where stars re - volve their lit - tle rounds.

2 Thee while the first archangel sings,
   He hides his face behind his wings;
   And ranks of shining thrones around
   Fall worshipping, and spread the ground.

3 Earth from afar hath heard Thy fame,
   And worms have learned to lisp Thy name:
   But O! the glories of Thy mind
   Leave all our soaring thoughts behind!

114.—WELTON. L. M.

Mrs. Voke.   Dr. Malan.

1. Sovereign of worlds I dis - play Thy power; Be this Thy Zi - on's fa - vored hour;
O bid the morn - ing star a - rise; O point the heathen to the skies.

2 Set up Thy throne where Satan reigns,
   In western wilds and eastern plains;
   Far let the gospel's sound be known;
   Make Thou the universe Thine own.

3 Speak, and the world shall hear Thy voice;
   Speak, and the desert shall rejoice:
   Dispel the gloom of heathen night;
   Bid every nation hail the light.

* From "Starry Crown," by per. W. A. Pond & Co.

116.—ARLINGTON. C. M.

WATTS.   DR. ARNE.

1. When I can read my title clear To mansions in the skies,
I'll bid farewell to every fear, And wipe my weeping eyes.

2. Should earth against my soul engage, And fiery darts be hurled,
Then I can smile at Satan's rage, And face a frowning world.

3 Let cares, like a wild deluge, come,
   Let storms of sorrow fall;
So I but safely reach my home,
   My God, my heaven, my all.

4 There I shall bathe my weary soul
   In seas of heavenly rest,
And not a wave of trouble roll
   Across my peaceful breast.

117.—AVON. C. M.

WATTS.   HUGH WILSON.

1. Am I a soldier of the cross, A follower of the Lamb? And shall I
fear to own His cause, Or blush to speak His name?

2. Must I be carried to the skies On flowery beds of ease, While others
fought to win the prize, And sail'd thro' bloody seas?

3 Are there no foes for me to face?
   Must I not stem the flood?
Is this vile world a friend to grace,
   To help me on to God?

4 Sure I must fight, if I would reign;
   Increase my courage, Lord;
I'll bear the toil, endure the pain,
   Supported by Thy word.

5 Thy saints in all this glorious war
   Shall conquer though they die;
They see the triumph from afar,
   And seize it with their eye.

6 When that illustrious day shall rise,
   And all Thy armies shine
In robes of victory thro' the skies,
   The glory shall be Thine.

118.—FOOTSTEPS OF JESUS.

Mrs. M. B. C. Slade. Dr. A. B. Everett.*

2 Tho' they lead o'er the cold, dark mountains,
   Seeking His sheep;
   Or along by Siloam's fountains,
   Helping the weak.—Cho.

3 If they lead through the temple holy,
   Preaching the word;
   Or in homes of the poor and lowly,
   Serving the Lord.—Cho.

4 Tho', dear Lord, in Thy pathway keeping,
   We follow Thee;
   Thro' the gloom of that sad place weeping,
   Gethsemane!—Cho.

5 If Thy way and its sorrows bearing,
   We go again,
   Up the slope of the hill-side, bearing
   Our cross of pain.—Cho.

6 By and by, through the shining portals,
   Turning our feet,
   We shall walk with the glad immortals
   Heaven's golden streets.—Cho.

7 Then at last when on high He sees us,
   Our journey done,
   We will rest where the steps of Jesus
   End at His throne.—Cho.

* By permission of R. M. McIntosh.

2 'Twas grace that taught my heart to fear,
And grace my fears relieved;
How precious did that grace appear
The hour I first believed!

3 Through many dangers, toils, and snares,
I have already come;
'Tis grace has brought me safe thus far,
And grace will lead me home.

4 The Lord has promised good to me—
His word my hope secures;
He will my shield and portion be
As long as life endures.

5 Yea, when this heart and flesh shall fail,
And mortal life shall cease,
I shall possess, within the veil,
A life of joy and peace.

121.—I LOVE TO TELL THE STORY. 7s & 6s.

Miss Kate Hankey.   William G. Fischer. *By per.*

1. I love to tell the sto-ry Of unseen things above, Of Jesus and His glo-ry, Of Je-sus and His love. I love to tell the sto-ry, Because I know 'tis true; It sat-isfies my longings, As nothing else can do.

2. I love to tell the sto-ry; More wonderful it seems Than all the golden fancies Of all our golden dreams. I love to tell the sto-ry, It did so much for me; And that is just the rea-son I tell it now to thee.

CHORUS.

I love to tell the sto-ry, 'Twill be my theme in glory, To tell the old, old sto-ry Of Je-sus and His love.

3 I love to tell the story;
'Tis pleasant to repeat
What seems, each time I tell it,
More wonderfully sweet.
I love to tell the story;
For some have never heard
The message of salvation
From God's own holy word.

4 I love to tell the story;
For those who know it best
Seem hungering and thirsting
To hear it like the rest.
And when, in scenes of glory,
I sing the new, new song,
'Twill be the old, old story,
That I have loved so long.

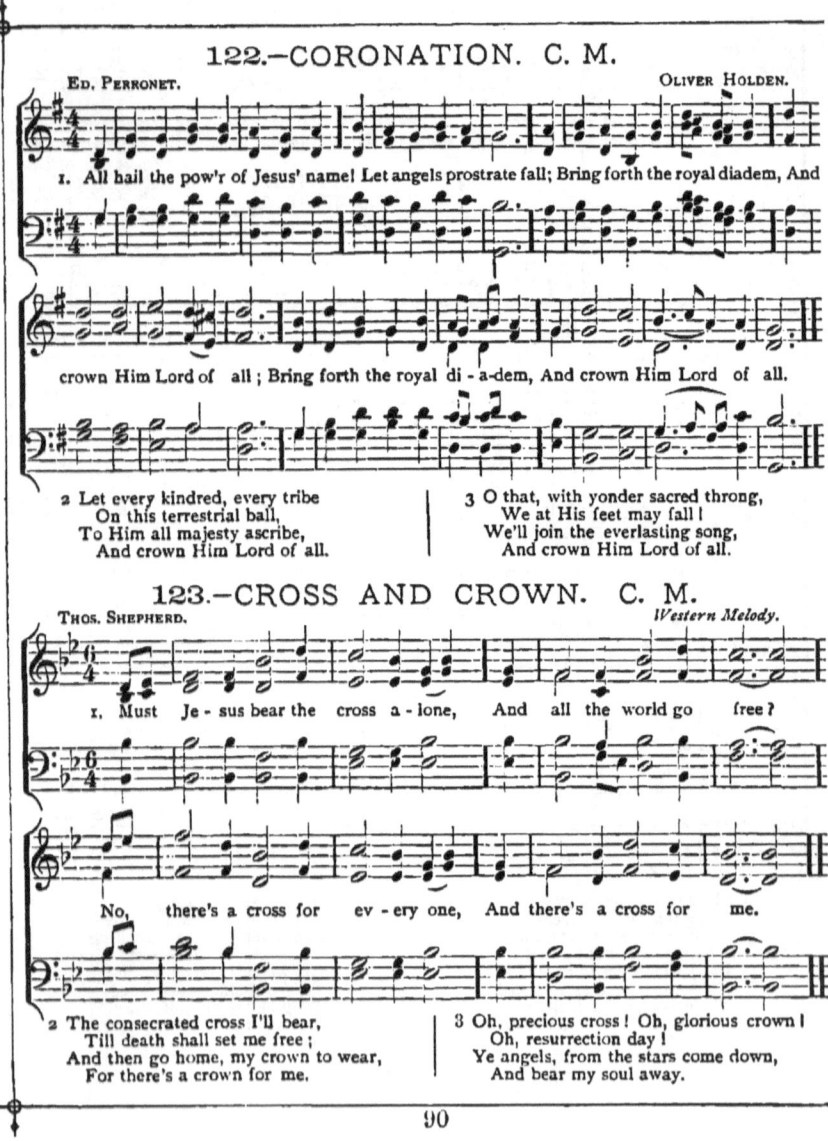

124.—THERE'LL BE JOY BY AND BY.

Mrs. E. C. Ellsworth. Rev. R. Lowry.*

1. Though the night be dark and drear-y, Though the way be long and wea-ry, Morn shall bring thee light and cheer; Child, look up, the dawn is near.

CHORUS.
There'll be joy by and by, There'll be joy by and by; In the dawn-ing of the morn-ing, There'll be joy by and by.

2 Though thine eyes are sad with weeping,
Through the night thy vigils keeping;
God shall wipe thy tears away,
Turn thy darkness into day.—Cho.

3 Though thy spirit faints with fasting
Through the hours so slowly wasting,
Morn shall bring a glorious feast,
Thou shalt sit an honored guest.—Cho.

* From "Welcome Tidings," by per. Biglow & Main, N. Y.

125.—DUNDEE. C. M.

Noel. *Scotch.*

1. If human kindness meets return, And owns the grateful tie; If tender thoughts within us burn To feel a friend is nigh.
2. O shall not warmer accents tell The grat-i-tude we owe To Him who died, our fears to quell, Our more than orphan's woe.

3 While yet His anguished soul surveyed
  Those pangs He would not flee,
  What love His latest words displayed,—
  " Meet and remember me!"

4 Remember Thee! Thy death, Thy shame,
  Our sinful hearts to share!
  O mem'ry, leave no other name
  But His recorded there!

126.—EVAN. C. M.

Havergal.

1. In mer-cy, Lord, re-mem-ber me, Through all the hours of night; And grant to me most gra-cious-ly The safe-guard of Thy might.

2 With cheerful heart I close mine eyes,
  Since Thou wilt not remove;
  O, in the morning let me rise,
  Rejoicing in Thy love.

3 Or, if this night should prove my last,
  And end my transient days;
  Lord, take me to Thy promised rest,
  Where I may sing Thy praise.

128.—GENEVA. C. M.

J. Addison.   J. Cole.

1. When all Thy mer-cies, O my God, My ris-ing soul sur-veys,
   Trans-port-ed with the view, I'm lost In won-der, love, and praise.

2 O how can words with equal warmth
  The gratitude declare
  That grows within my ravished heart?
  But Thou canst read it there!

3 Thy providence my life sustained,
  And all my wants redressed;
  With ashes who would grudge to part,
  When called on angels' bread to feast?

129.—GRIGG. C. M.

Watts.   J. Griggs, Jr.

1. So did the He-brew proph-et raise The bra-zen ser-pent high:
   The wound-ed felt im-me-diate ease, The camp for-bore to die.

[Balance of verses next page.]

130.—THE SWEET STORY.

Mrs. Jemima Luke. — English.

1 I THINK, when I read that sweet story of old,
   When Jesus was here among men,
   How he called little children as lambs to His fold,
   I should like to have been with Him then.

2 I wish that His hands had been placed on my head,
   That His arms had been thrown around me;
   That I might have seen His kind look when He said,
   "Let the little ones come unto me."

3 Yet still to His footstool in prayer I may go,
   And ask for a share in His love;
   And if I thus earnestly seek Him below,
   I shall see Him and hear Him above:

4 In that beautiful place He has gone to prepare,
   For all who are washed and forgiven;
   And many dear children are gathering there,
   "For of such is the kingdom of heaven."

GRIGG—Concluded.

2 "Look upward in the dying hour,
   And live!" the prophet cries!
   But Christ performs a nobler cure,
   When faith lifts up her eyes.

3 High on the cross the Saviour hung!
   High in the heavens He reigns!
   Here sinners, by th' old serpent stung,
   Look, and forget their pains.

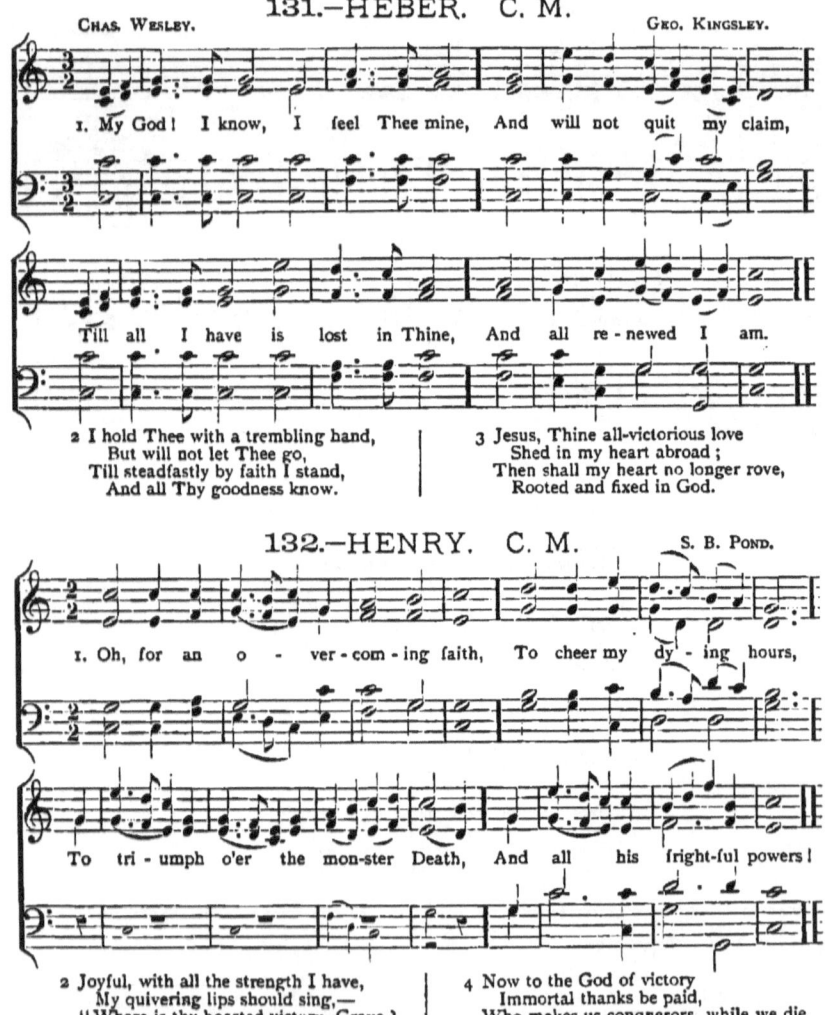

133.—RESCUE THE PERISHING.

FANNY J. CROSBY. W. H. DOANE.*

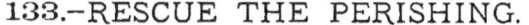

1. Res - cue the per-ish-ing, Care for the dy - ing, Snatch them in pit - y from sin and the grave; Weep o'er the err - ing one, Lift up the fall - en, Tell them of Je - sus, the might - y to save. Res - cue the per - ish-ing, Care for the dy - ing, Je - sus is mer - ci - ful, Je - sus will save.

2. Tho' they are slighting Him, Still He is wait - ing, Wait - ing the pen - i - tent child to re-ceive; Plead with them ear-nest - ly, Plead with them gen - tly, He will for - give if they on - ly be - lieve.

CHORUS.

3 Down in the human heart,
   Crushed by the tempter,
Feelings lie buried that grace can restore;
   Touched by a loving heart,
   Wakened by kindness,
Chords that were broken will vibrate once
    more.

4 Rescue the perishing,
   Duty demands it ;
Strength for thy labor the Lord will provide ;
   Back to the narrow way
   Patiently win them ;
Tell the poor wanderer a Saviour has
    died.

* *From "Pure Gold," by per. of Biglow & Main, N. Y.*

134.—MANOAH. C. M.

DODDRIDGE.   ROSSINI.

1. Do not I love Thee, O my Lord? Be-hold my heart, and see;
2. Do not I love Thee from my soul? Then let me noth-ing love;
And turn each curs-ed i-dol out That dares to ri-val Thee....
Dead be my heart to ev-ery joy. When Je-sus can-not move....

3 Hast Thou a lamb in all Thy flock
   I would disdain to feed?
   Hast Thou a foe before whose face
   I fear Thy cause to plead?

4 Thou know'st I love Thee, dearest Lord;
   But O! I long to soar
   Far from the sphere of mortal joys,
   And learn to love Thee more.

135.—MARLOW. C. M.

ANDREW REED.   DR. L. MASON.

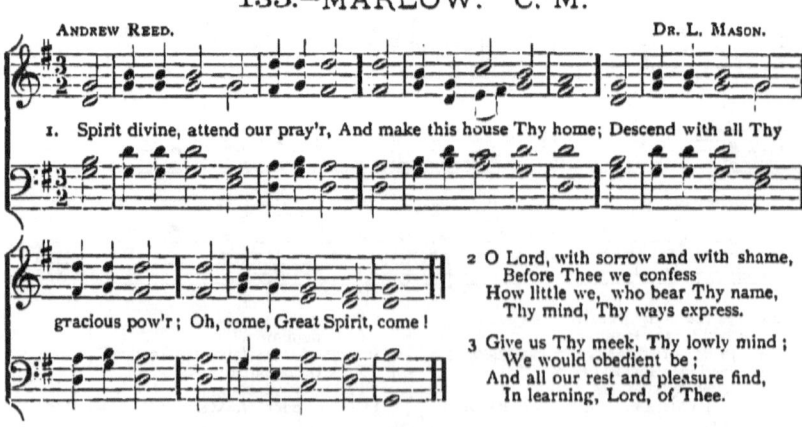

1. Spirit divine, attend our pray'r, And make this house Thy home; Descend with all Thy gracious pow'r; Oh, come, Great Spirit, come!

2 O Lord, with sorrow and with shame,
   Before Thee we confess
   How little we, who bear Thy name,
   Thy mind, Thy ways express.

3 Give us Thy meek, Thy lowly mind;
   We would obedient be;
   And all our rest and pleasure find,
   In learning, Lord, of Thee.

136.—THE GOLDEN STORE.

From "Song Sermons," by per.—PHILIP PHILLIPS.

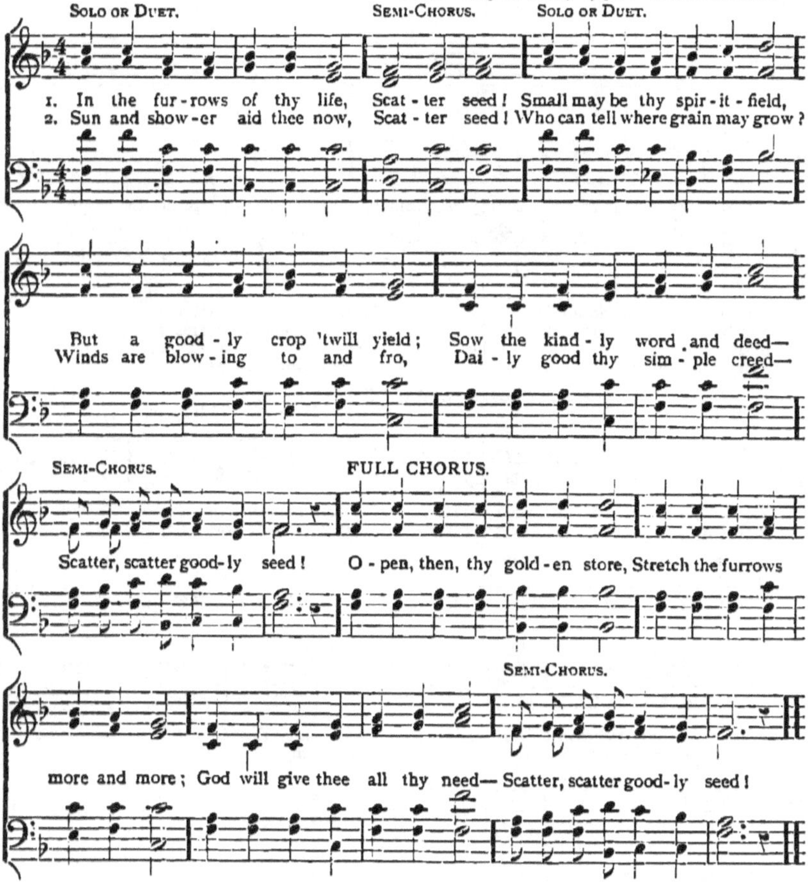

1. In the fur-rows of thy life, Scat-ter seed! Small may be thy spir-it-field, But a good-ly crop 'twill yield; Sow the kind-ly word and deed—Scatter, scatter good-ly seed! O-pen, then, thy gold-en store, Stretch the furrows more and more; God will give thee all thy need— Scatter, scatter good-ly seed!

2. Sun and show-er aid thee now, Scat-ter seed! Who can tell where grain may grow? Winds are blow-ing to and fro, Dai-ly good thy sim-ple creed—

3 Though thy work should seem to fail,
　Scatter seed !
Some may fall on stony ground :
Flower and blade are often found
In the clefts we little heed ;
Scatter, scatter goodly seed !—CHO.

4 Spring-time always dawns for thee !
　Scatter seed !
Open, then, thy golden store,
Stretch thy furrows more and more ;
God will give thee all thy need ;
Scatter, scatter goodly seed !—CHO.

2 And thou, refulgent orb of day,
In brighter flames arrayed,
My soul, that springs beyond thy sphere,
No more demands thy aid.

3 The Father of eternal light
Shall there His beams display;
Nor shall one moment's darkness mix
With that unvaried day.

3 What peaceful hours I once enjoyed!
How sweet their mem'ry still!
But they have left an aching void
The world can never fill.

4 Return, O holy Dove, return,
Sweet messenger of rest!
I hate the sins that made Thee mourn,
And drove Thee from my breast.

139.—URGE THEM TO COME.

Dr. C. R. Blackall.   W. H. Doane.

1. In the highways and hedges go seek for the lost, Gather them in-to the fold—
2. If the Shepherd we love, we must care for the sheep; Precious are they in His sight;

Was the earnest command that our Saviour divine Taught His dis-ci-ples of old.
They are out in the desert, they wander a-lone; Lead them from darkness to light.

CHORUS.

Urge them to come, Show them the way, Ten-der-ly, lov-ing-ly, bring them to-day;

Urge them to come, Why should they roam? Bring them along to our dear Sabbath home.

3 To the weary and thirsty the Saviour has said,
"Come, heavy-laden, to me,
I will give you to drink of the water of life;"
Tell them the fountain is free.—Cho.

4 There's a welcome for all in the kingdom of
All who repent and believe;   [grace,
And the souls that have strayed and returned
to the fold,
Jesus will gladly receive.—Cho.

* *From "Pure Gold," by per. of Biglow & Main, N. Y.*

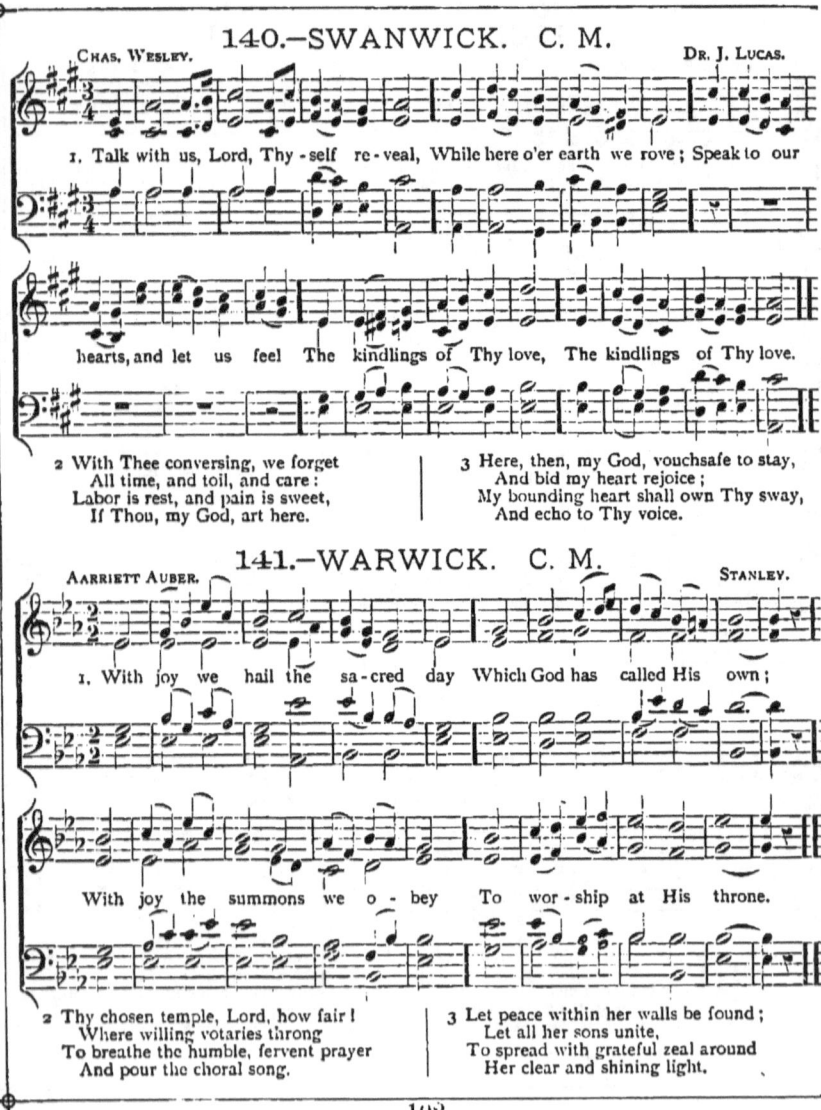

142.—PENITENCE. 7s, 6s & 8s.

CHAS. WESLEY.   OAKLEY.

1. Jesus, let Thy pitying eye Call back a wand'ring sheep;
False to Thee, like Peter, I Would fain, like Peter, weep.
Let me be by grace restored; On me be all long-suff'ring shown:
Turn, and look upon me, Lord, And break my heart of stone.

2 See me, Saviour, from above,
  Nor suffer me to die!
Life, and happiness, and love,
  Drop from Thy gracious eye:
Speak the reconciling word,
  And let Thy mercy melt me down:
Turn, and look upon me, Lord,
  And break my heart of stone.

3 Look as when thy languid eye
  Was closed that we might live:
"Father," (at the point to die
  My Saviour gasped,) "forgive!"
Surely with that dying word
  He turns, and looks, and cries, "'Tis done!"
O my bleeding, loving Lord,
  Thou break'st my heart of stone!

143.—WOODLAND. C. M.

Tappan.   N. D. Gould.

1. There is an hour of peaceful rest, To mourning wand'rers given; There is a joy for souls distress'd, A balm for ev-ery wounded breast,—'Tis found a-bove in heaven.

2 There is a home for weary souls
By sin and sorrow driven,
When tossed on life's tempestuous shoals,
Where storms arise and ocean rolls,
And all is drear; 'tis heaven.

3 There faith lifts up the tearless eye,
To brighter prospects given;
And views the tempest passing by,
The evening shadows quickly fly,
And all serene in heaven.

144.—ZERAH. C. M.

Chas. Wesley.   Dr. L. Mason.

1. Hail, Father, Son, and Holy Ghost, One God in persons three, Of Thee we make our joyful boast, And homage pay to Thee; Of Thee we make our joyful boast, And homage pay to Thee.

2 Present alike in every place,
Thy Godhead we adore;
Beyond the bounds of time and space
Thou dwellest evermore.

3 Wherefore let every creature give
To Thee the praise designed;
But chiefly, Lord, the thanks receive,
The hearts, of all mankind.

145.—BETHANY.

ADAMS.   DR. L. MASON.

1. Nearer, my God, to Thee, Nearer to Thee, E'en though it be a cross, That raiseth me; Still all my song shall be, Nearer, my God, to Thee, Nearer, my God, to Thee, Nearer to Thee.

2 Though like the wanderer,
   The sun gone down,
Darkness be over me,
   My rest a stone ;
Yet in my dreams I'd be
Nearer, my God, to Thee,
   Nearer to Thee.

3 There let the way appear
   Steps unto heaven ;
All that Thou sendest me
   In mercy given ;
Angels to beckon me
Nearer, my God, to Thee,
   Nearer to Thee.

4 Then with my waking thoughts
   Bright with Thy praise,
Out of my stony griefs
   Altars I'll raise ;
So by my woes to be
Nearer, my God, to Thee,
   Nearer to Thee.

5 Or if on joyful wing,
   Cleaving the sky,
Sun, moon, and stars forgot,
   Upward I fly,
Still all my song shall be
Nearer, my God, to Thee,
   Nearer to Thee.

2 See heathen nations bending
   Before the God we love,
   And thousand hearts ascending
     In gratitude above ;
   While sinners, now confessing,
   The gospel call obey,
   And seek the Saviour's blessing,
     A nation in a day.

3 Blest river of salvation,
   Pursue thine onward way ;
   Flow thou to every nation,
     Nor in thy richness stay :
   Stay not till all the lowly
   Triumphant reach thy home :
   Stay not till all the holy
     Proclaim, "The Lord is come !"

2 He framed the globe ; He built the sky ;
  He made the shining worlds on high,
    And reigns in glory there :
  His beams are majesty and light ;
  His beauties, how divinely bright !
    His dwelling-place, how fair !

3 Come the great day, the glorious hour,
  When earth shall feel His saving power,
    All nations fear His name :
  Then shall the race of men confess
  The beauty of His holiness,
    His saving grace proclaim.

ALPHABETICAL INDEX.

Names.	Nos.
Antioch	1
After the Harvest	65
Ain	109
Amsterdam	3
Angel Watchers	83
Ariel	8
Arlington	116
Around the Throne	92
Assurance	106
Autumn	5
Avon	117
Balerma	119
Beautiful Valley of Eden	68
Belief	11
Belton	60
Bemerton	120
Bethany	145
Boylston	61
Christmas Morn	28
Colquit	54
Come, ye disconsolate	14
Come unto Me	30
Consecration	43
Contrast	12
Coronation	122
Cross and Crown	123
Dennis	63
Dover	64
Duke Street	84
Dundee	125
Evan	126

Names.	Nos.
Even Me	35
Every day and hour	62
Effingham	85
Eshtemoa	44
Federal Street	87
Flow on, Sweet Stream	74
Footsteps of Jesus	118
Forest	88
Gathering Home	100
Gather the Children	32
Geneva	128
Gerar	66
Golden Hill	67
Glory to God	42
Greenville	15
Grigg	129
Haddam	17
Hail, thou once-despised Jesus	6
Hastings	19
Heber	131
Hebron	90
Hendon	46
Henry	132
His love is ever o'er us	10
Home, Sweet Home	95
Homeward Bound	13
Horton	47
Hosanna	23
How calm and beautiful the morn	20
Iddo	112
I love to tell the story	121

ALPHABETICAL INDEX.

Names.	Nos.
Jesus, be near me	16
Judd	69
Kingsley	22
Laban	72
Lenox	26
Lisbon	70
Lischer	24
Loving Kindness	98
Luther	73
Lyons	27
Manoah	134
Marching Home	71
Marlow	135
Martyn	51
Mendon	93
Meribah	147
Merton	137
Migdol	91
Mighty Lord, extend Thine Empire	34
Missionary Chant	94
Missionary Hymn	29
Nettleton	31
O! Glorious Hope	9
Old Hundred	97
Oliphant	33
Olney	75
Onido	49
Orland	96
Ortonville	138
Ozrem	76
Park Street	99
Pass me not	50
Penitence	142
Praise the Lord	59
Precious Name	127
Protection	103
Rejoice! Rejoice!	4
Rescue the Perishing	133
Rest	104
Retreat	101
River of Song	89

Names.	Nos.
Rockingham	105
Rock of Ages	52
Rosefield	53
Rothwell	102
Sabbath	55
Saint Thomas	78
Saved every moment	56
Save, Lord, or we perish	25
Shirland	81
Sicily	37
Silver Street	79
Solitude	57
Stonefield	107
Swanwick	140
Tamworth	38
To-day	36
The Blessed Mercy-Seat	45
The Blissful Home	7
The Gate Ajar	77
The Golden Store	136
The Kingdom Coming	48
Then Hoist the Sails	21
The Prodigal	86
The Royal Diadem	115
There'll be Joy by-and-by	124
The Sweet Story	130
Trinity	58
Truro	108
Urge Them to Come	139
Uxbridge	110
Ware	111
Warwick	141
Watchman, tell us of the Night	39
Watchman (S. M.)	82
Webb	146
Wells	113
Welton	114
We'll Wait till Jesus Comes	18
What must it be to be there	80
Wilmot	40
Woodland	143
Zerah	144
Zion	41

{ 1846 }   THE   { 1879 }

ESTEY ORGAN

IS THE BEST

ON THE GLOBE

FOR

CONSERV ATORIES
SUNDAY SCHOOLS
LODGE ROOMS
SOCIE TIES
CHUR CHES
CHAP ELS

HOMES.

Address for Illustrated Catalogue,

J. ESTEY & COMPANY,

BRATTLEBORO, VT.

www.ingramcontent.com/pod-product-compliance
Lightning Source LLC
Chambersburg PA
CBHW020147170426
43199CB00010B/919